The Key to Scales & Arpeggios

for Piano Grades 3 and 4

A NEW method focusing on
simultaneous finger patterns

Simple Rules
Playing Hands Together is Effortless!
Keyboard Illustrations

Jane Mann

Sarah Quintin

Produced by
Alfred Publishing Co. (UK) Ltd.
Burnt Mill, Elizabeth Way, Harlow
Essex, CM20 2HX
alfreduk.com

Printed in the United Kingdom

ISBN-10: 1-4706-1220-8
ISBN-13: 978-1-4706-1220-7

Contents

Scales and Arpeggios are Great!

The simple rules and illustrations in this book make playing scales and arpeggios easy

You can learn to enjoy playing scales and arpeggios! They are important for exercising our fingers and improving technique just as athletes warm up their muscles. This method makes it easy to learn the shape and pattern of each key which will enable you to read and play music more fluently.

Based on traditional fingering, there are simple rules or anchor points which identify where LH and RH fingers play simultaneously. In this series of books the scales and arpeggios are arranged according to these finger pattern rules rather than the more usual circle of fifths order.

For example: Scales Group 1 contains 9 scales with the same rule:

'3rd fingers play together'

It's easy with this method! The rules will help you to learn quickly and securely, fixing the finger coordination.

Before playing, study the keyboard illustrations for faster learning.

For example, look at the scale of D major on page 12:

- Identify the rule: D major scale is '3rd fingers play together'.

- Notice that both 3rd fingers play F♯ and B.

- Check the differences between black and white note fingering.

- Which note is played with finger 4? This is where errors can occur, especially on descending.

Suddenly the scale is easier and you are ready to play.

Remember the rule - you can't go wrong!

Throughout each book, the circle of fifths is used to illustrate the fingering groups and page numbers.

Major and Minor Scales Explained

A scale is an octave of various tones and semitones.

Tones and Semitones in scales

Major	T	T	S	T	T	T	S
Harmonic Minor	T	S	T	T	S	2	S

↓

(Jump over 2 notes)

Major and minor scales are closely related.
They share the same key signature and many of the same notes.

For example:

- Play the scale of G major.
- Now play it again, and lower the 3rd and 6th notes a semitone, i.e. lower B and E down to B♭ and E♭.
- This is the scale of G harmonic minor.
- G minor shares the same key signature as B♭ major.
  Can you see how similar they are?

Minor scales begin **3 semitones below** the related major tonic note.

B♭ major - count **down** 3 semitones - G minor.

Remember: '**Miners** (minors) go **DOWN** to dig!'

The Major Scale Groups

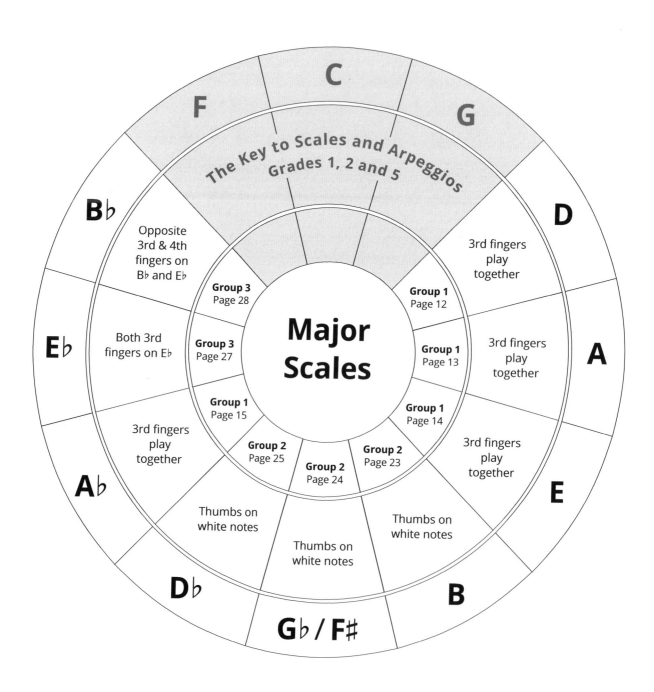

The circle of fifths order of the sharps and flats:

♯ **F**ather **C**hristmas **G**ave **D**ad **A**n **E**lectric **B**lanket
♭ **B**lanket **E**xploded **A**nd **D**ad **G**ot **C**old **F**eet

The Minor Scale Groups

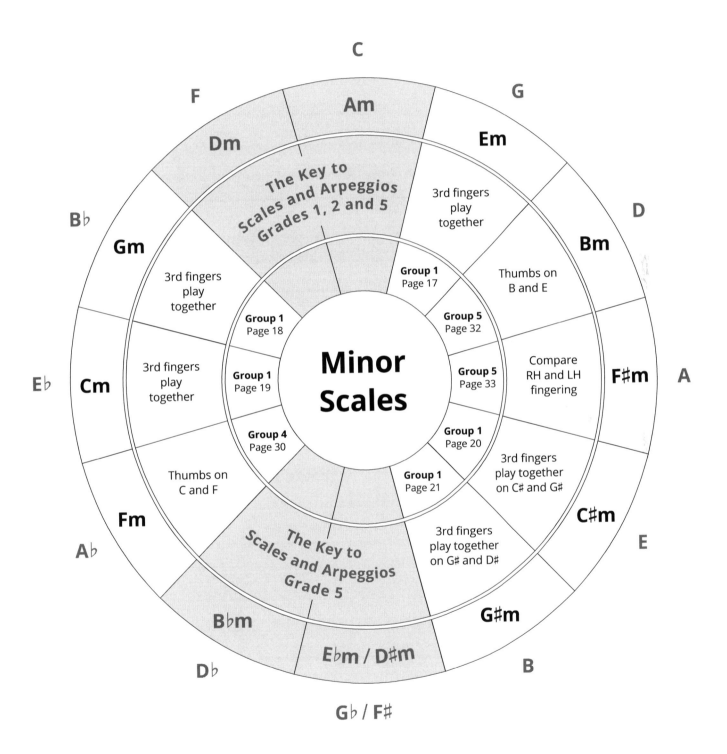

Melodic minor scales are not included.

The fingering is the same apart from the scales of B♭ minor and F# minor.

The Major Arpeggio Groups

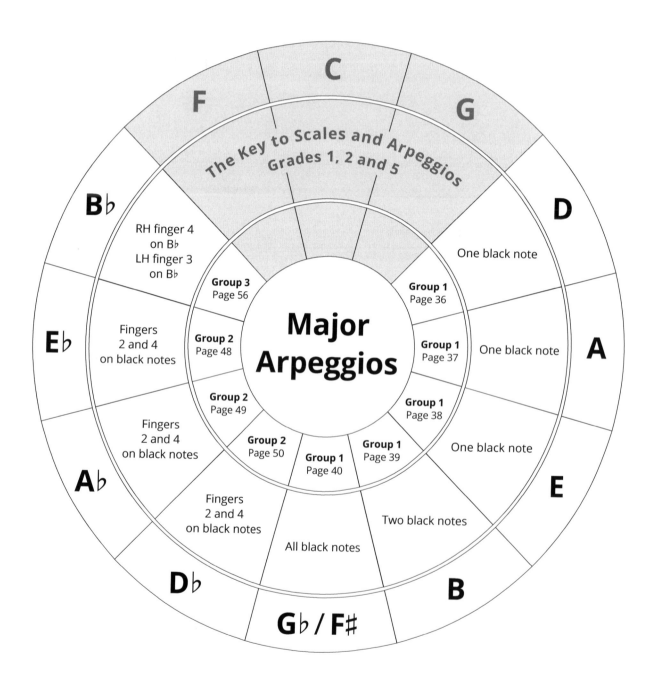

The Minor Arpeggio Groups

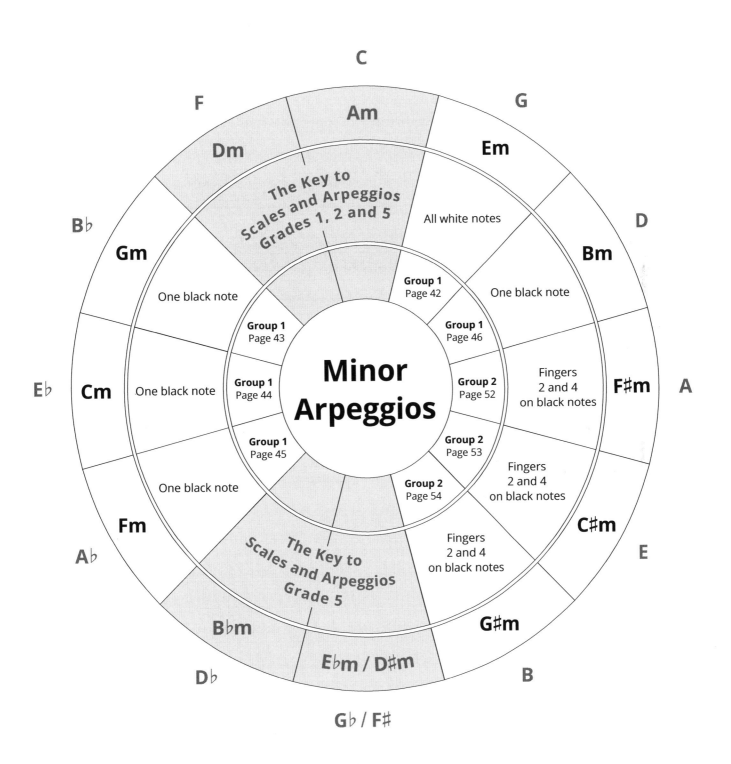

How to Practise

Accurate and repeated practice fixes the muscle memory. It works!
Be patient as it may take longer than you expect.

We need to play scales and arpeggios so that they become fixed and automatic.
It only takes a few minutes to play a scale 10 times - shorter practice twice a day
is more beneficial than one long practice.

How to practise:

1. Learn one octave **SLOWLY** with separate hands.

2. Learn two octaves with separate hands.

3. Play one octave with both hands together, gradually increasing the speed
   and **watch your hands** while playing.

   Repeat steps 1, 2 and 3 until the fingering becomes automatic.

4. Now play two octaves with both hands together slowly. It is important to
   play **slowly enough** for **complete accuracy** to fix the muscle memory.

5. Accuracy is more important than speed.

6. Vary your practice with legato, staccato, *forte* and *piano.*

Tips:

Begin with the **descending** scale or arpeggio for more secure fingering.

Test yourself on the fingering rule before starting each scale.

Watch continually for the correct finger pattern, especially on descending.

Listen for an even tone and clear legato sound.

Create flashcards for each scale, arpeggio, etc. Shuffle, then place the
pile face down at the end of the keyboard. Turn over the top card and play
whichever exercise is shown. This avoids the tendency to practise in the same
order each time.

Major Scales
Group 1

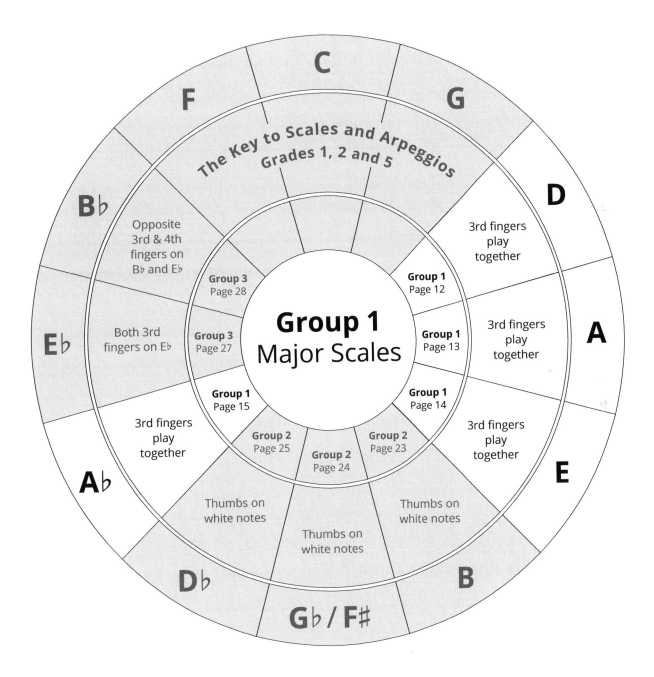

The Key to Scales and Arpeggios
Grades 1, 2 and 5

Group 1
Major Scales

C F G Bb D Eb A Ab E Db B Gb/F#

Opposite 3rd & 4th fingers on Bb and Eb

Both 3rd fingers on Eb

3rd fingers play together (×4)

Thumbs on white notes (×3)

Group 1 Page 12
Group 1 Page 13
Group 1 Page 14
Group 1 Page 15
Group 2 Page 23
Group 2 Page 24
Group 2 Page 25
Group 3 Page 27
Group 3 Page 28

Tips:

- **Look** for the tones and semitones as you play.
- **Play the tonic chord** before each scale.

D major

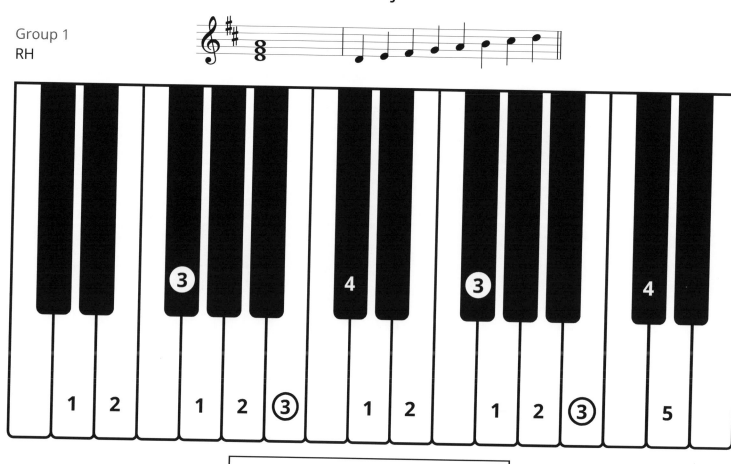

3rd fingers play together

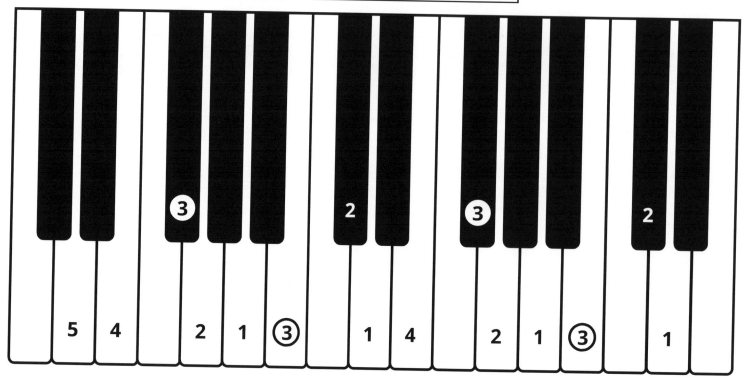

LH

A major

Group 1
RH

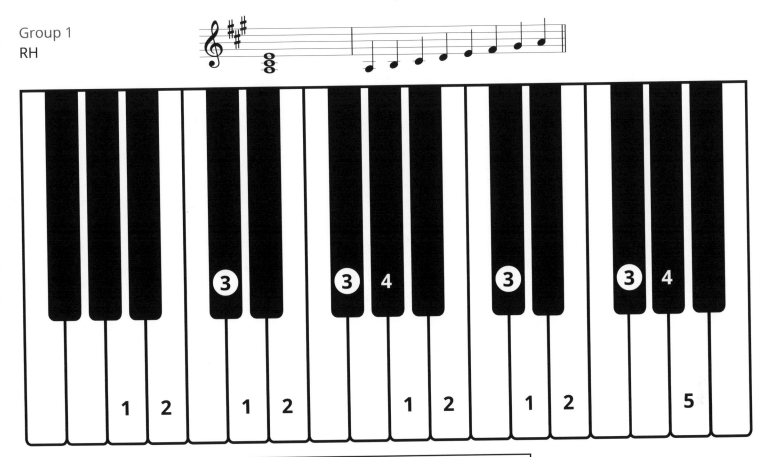

1   2   1   2   1   2   1   2   5

3rd fingers play together

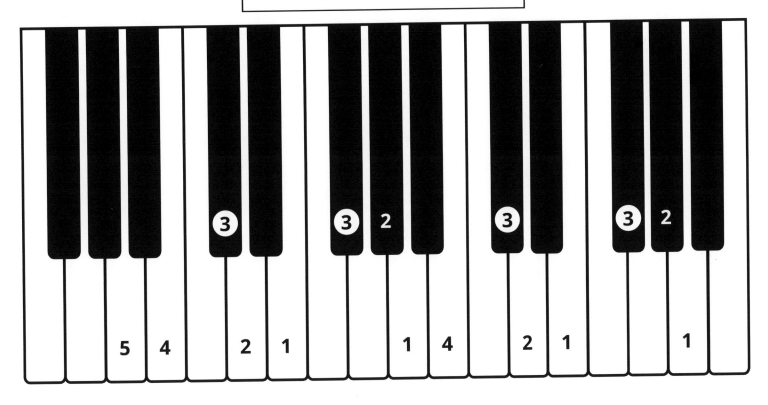

5   4   2   1   1   4   2   1   1

LH

E major

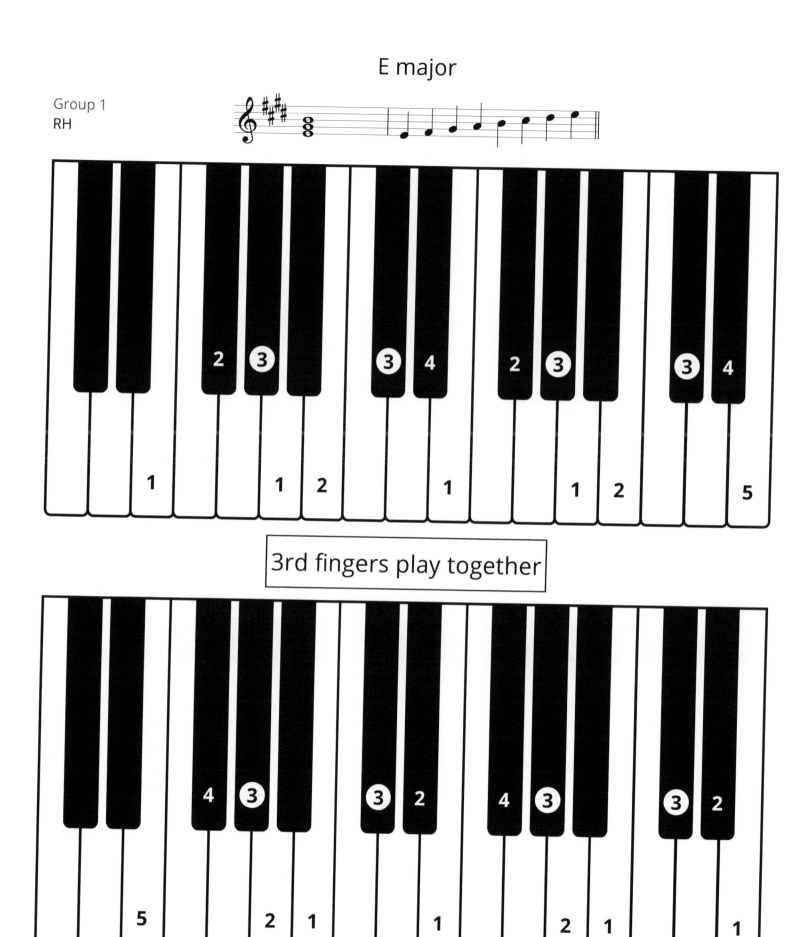

3rd fingers play together

LH

A♭ major

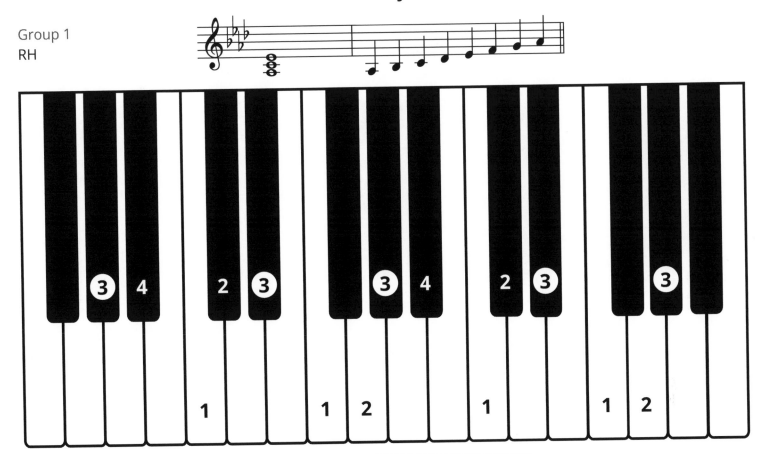

3rd fingers play together

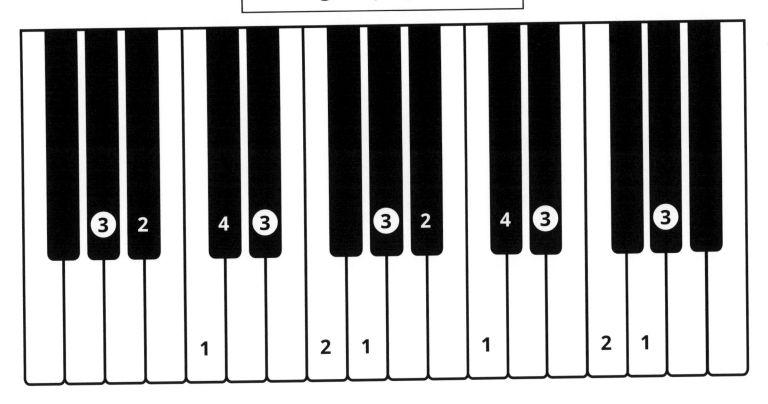

LH

Minor Scales
Group 1

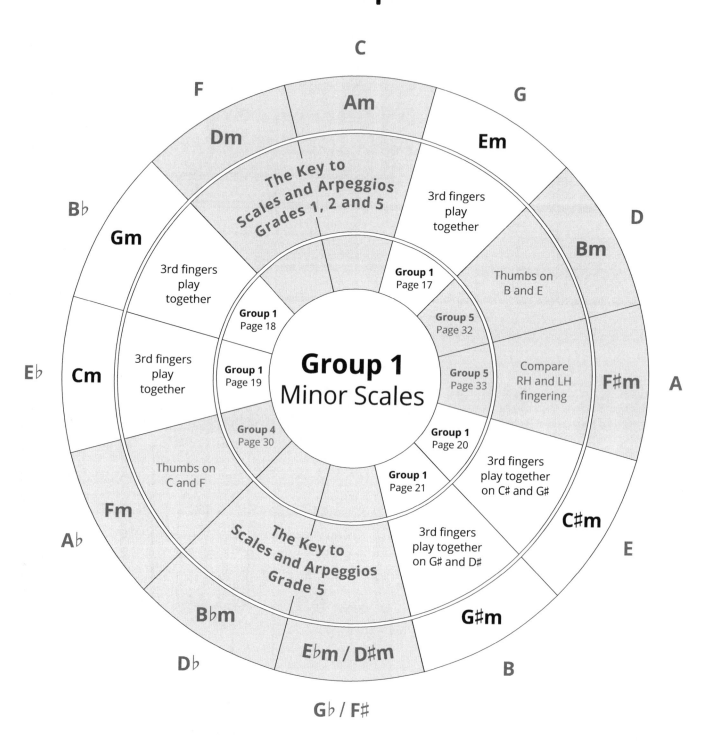

E harmonic minor

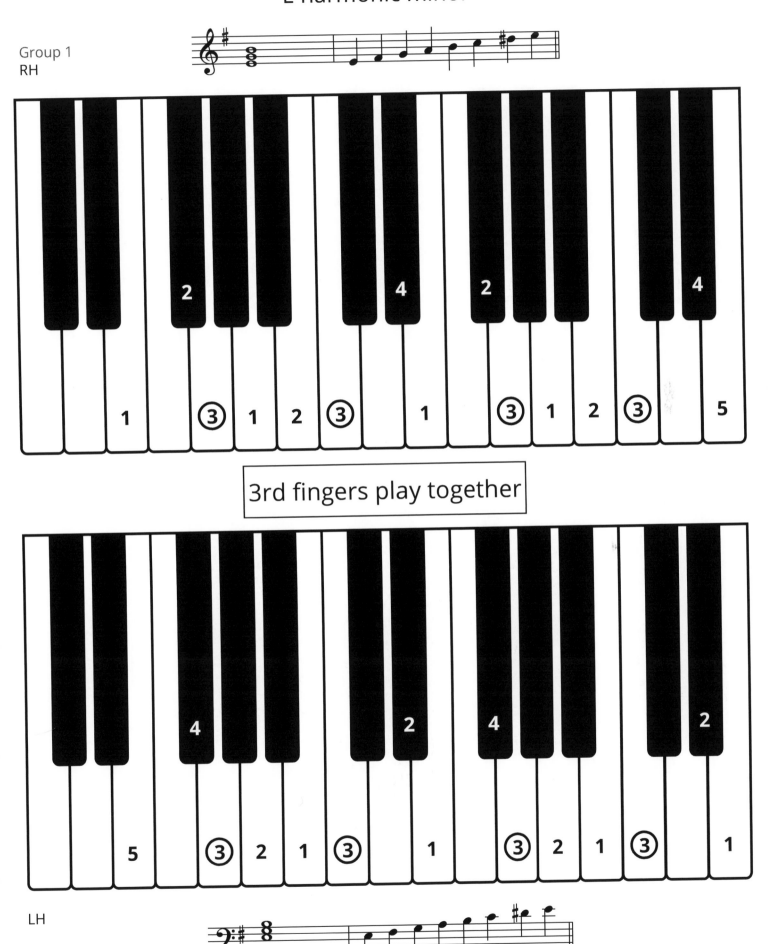

3rd fingers play together

LH

G harmonic minor

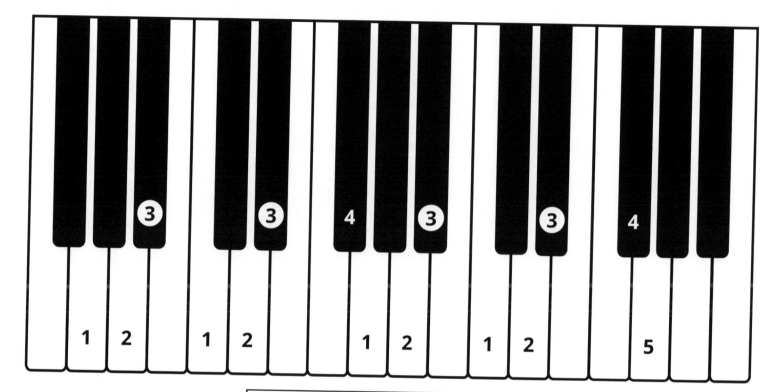

3rd fingers play together

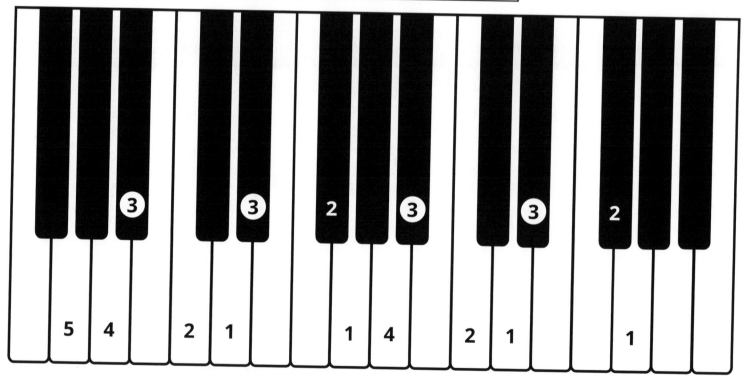

LH

C harmonic minor

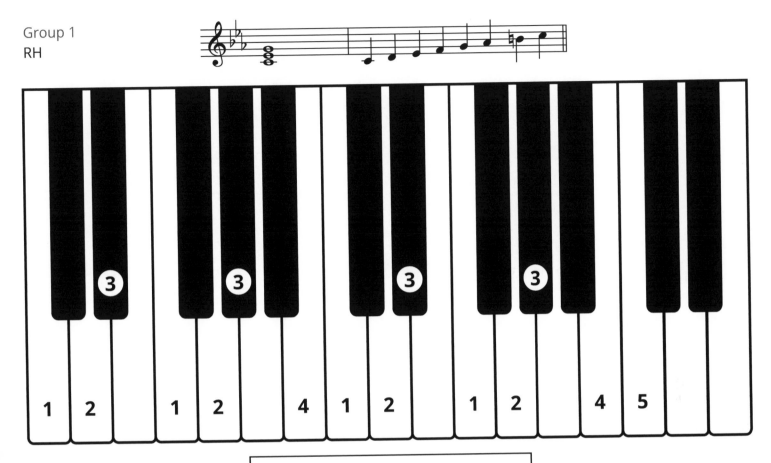

3rd fingers play together

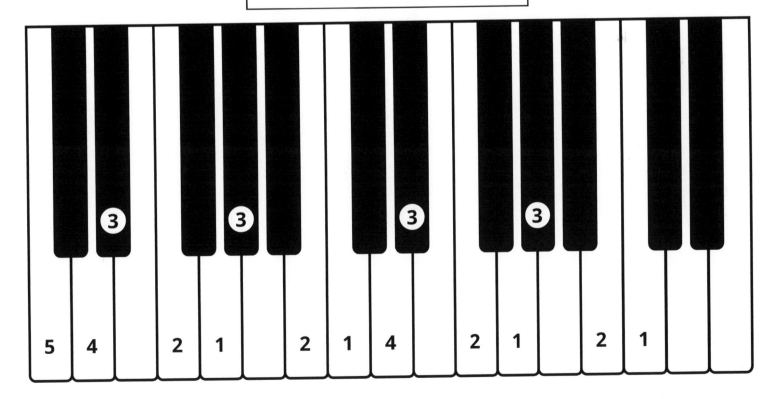

LH

Enharmonic D♭

C# harmonic minor

Group 1
RH

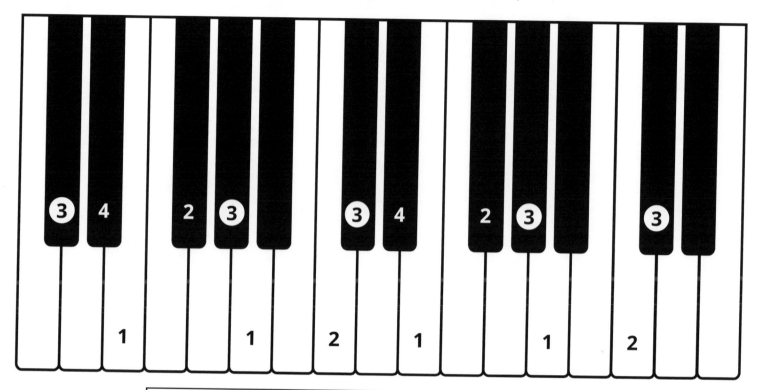

3rd fingers play together on C# and G#

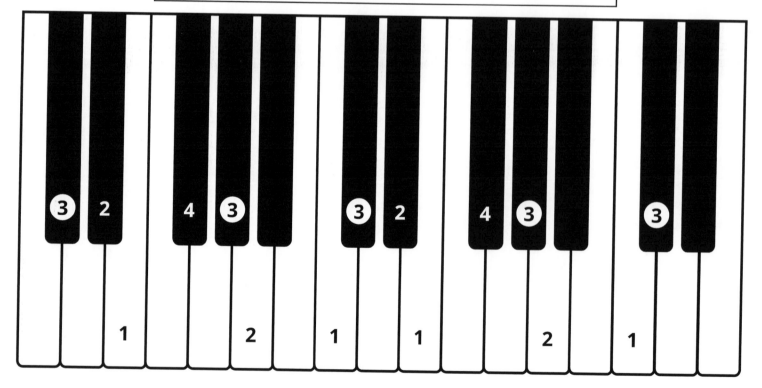

LH

Enharmonic A♭

G# harmonic minor

Group 1
RH

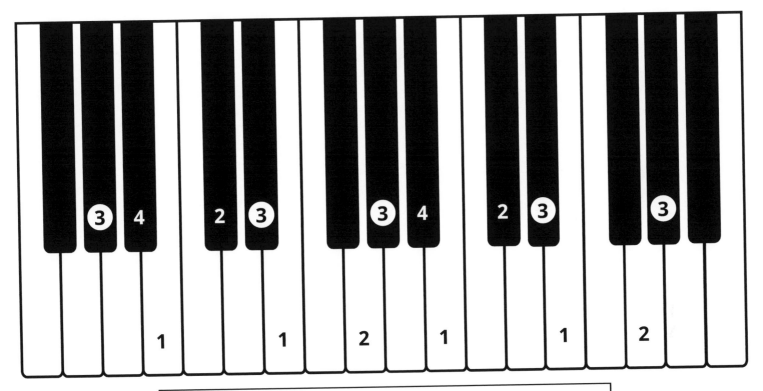

3rd fingers play together on G# and D#

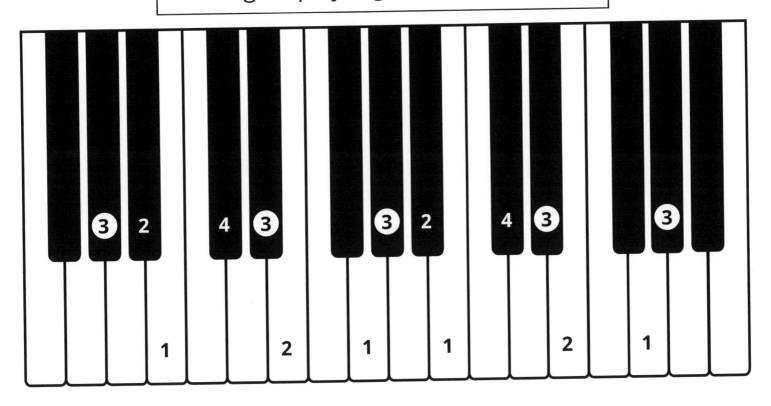

LH

Major Scales
Group 2

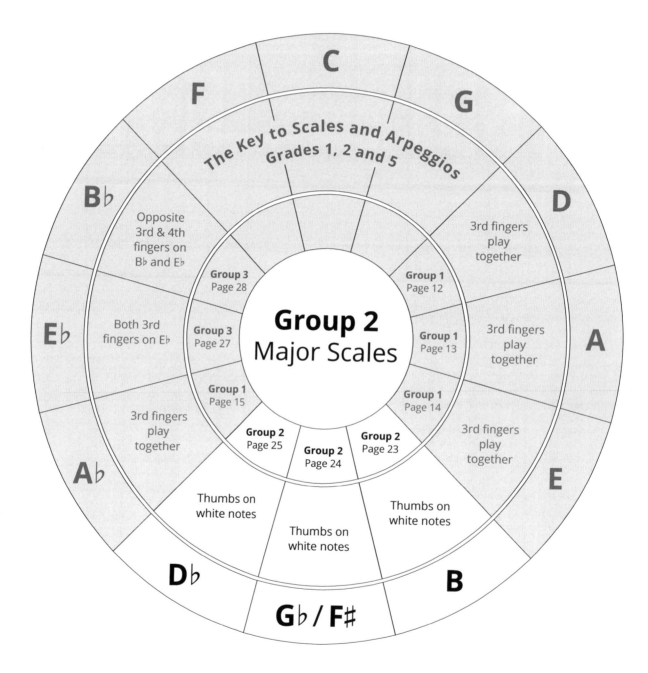

The Key to Scales and Arpeggios
Grades 1, 2 and 5

Group 2
Major Scales

C · F · G · Bb · D · Eb · A · Ab · E · Db · B · Gb / F#

Group 1 Page 12
Group 1 Page 13
Group 1 Page 14
Group 1 Page 15
Group 3 Page 27
Group 3 Page 28
Group 2 Page 23
Group 2 Page 24
Group 2 Page 25

Opposite 3rd & 4th fingers on Bb and Eb

Both 3rd fingers on Eb

3rd fingers play together

3rd fingers play together

3rd fingers play together

3rd fingers play together

3rd fingers play together

Thumbs on white notes

Thumbs on white notes

Thumbs on white notes

Tip:

- Check the semitones between 3/4 and 7/8 for the correct white notes.

B major

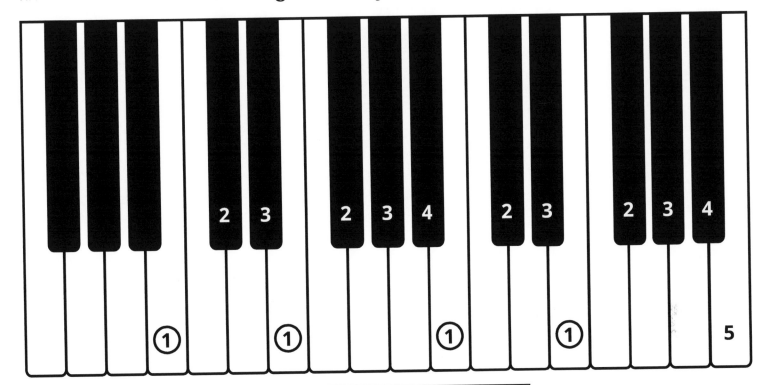

Thumbs on white notes

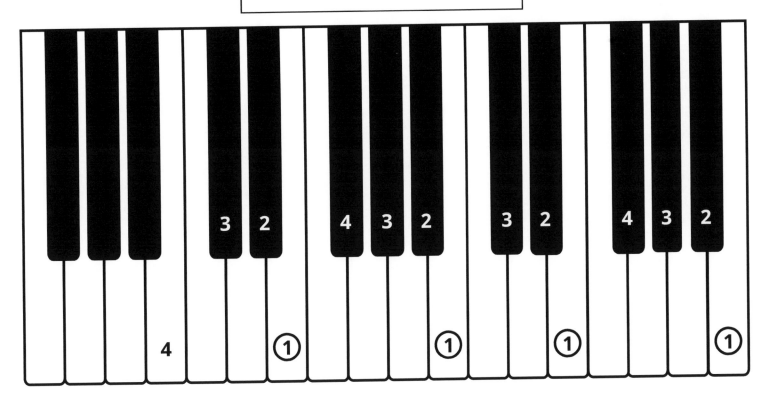

LH

F# major

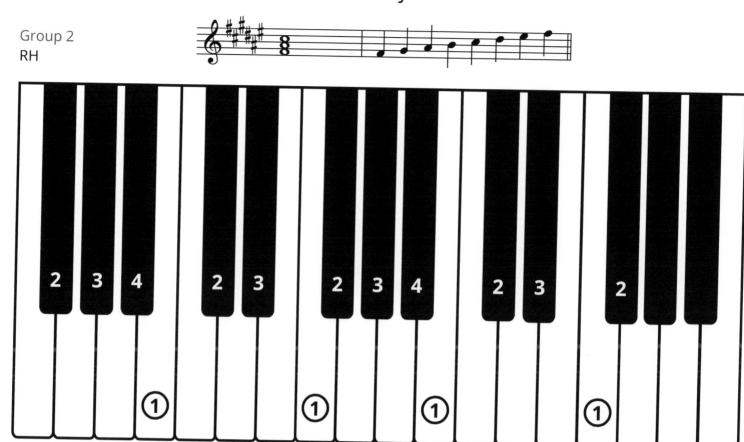

Thumbs on white notes

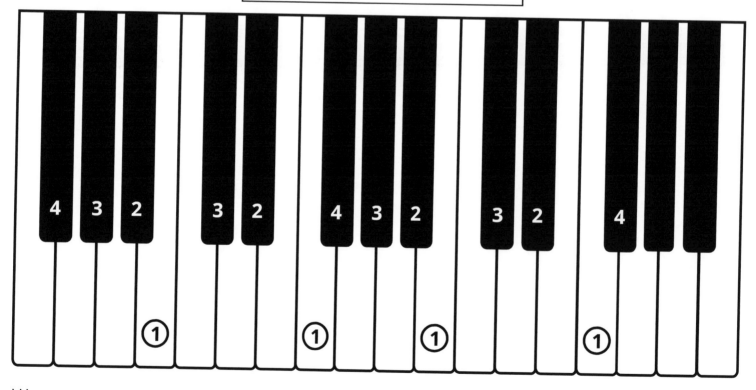

LH

Db major

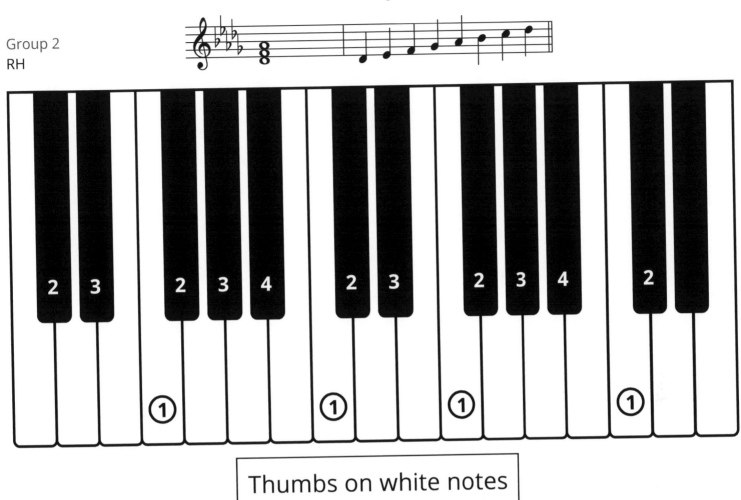

Thumbs on white notes

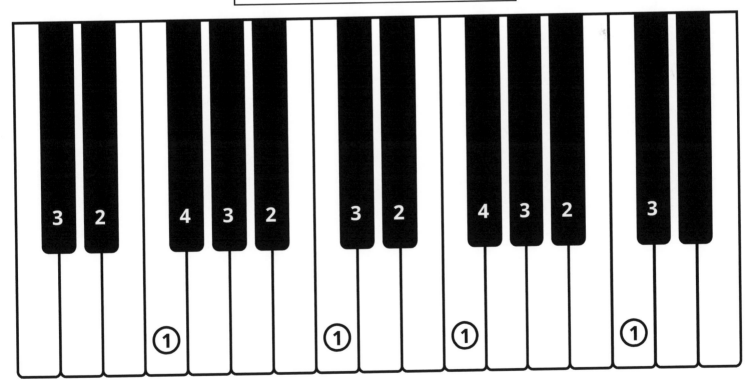

LH

Major Scales
Group 3

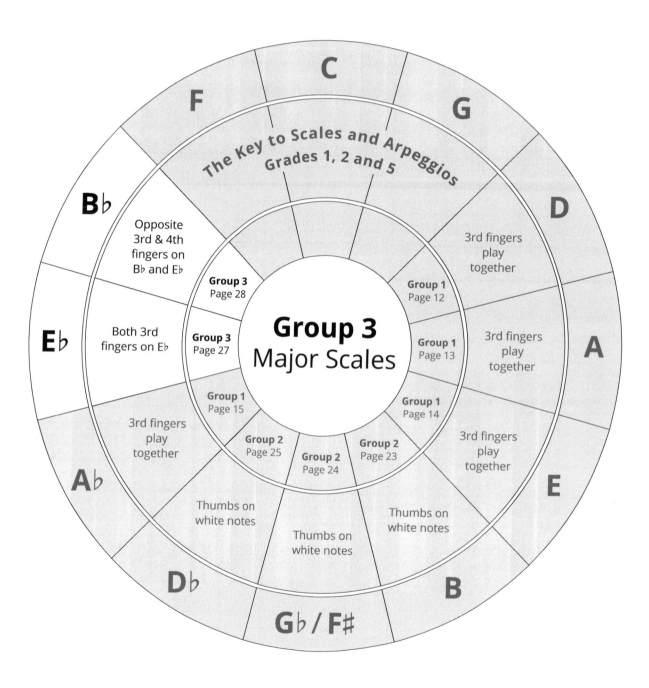

The Key to Scales and Arpeggios
Grades 1, 2 and 5

Group 3
Major Scales

C
G
D
A
E
B
Gb / F#
Db
Ab
Eb
Bb
F

Opposite 3rd & 4th fingers on Bb and Eb

Both 3rd fingers on Eb

Group 3
Page 28

Group 3
Page 27

Group 1
Page 15

Group 2
Page 25

Group 2
Page 24

Group 2
Page 23

Group 1
Page 14

Group 1
Page 13

Group 1
Page 12

3rd fingers play together

3rd fingers play together

3rd fingers play together

3rd fingers play together

Thumbs on white notes

Thumbs on white notes

Thumbs on white notes

E♭ major

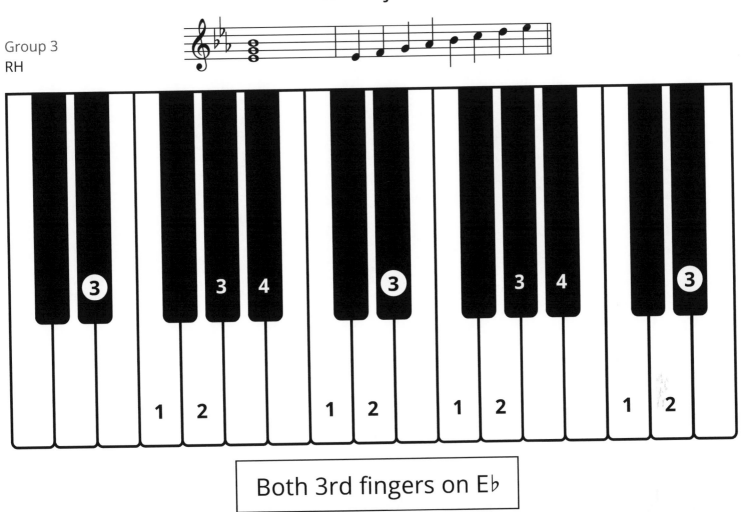

Both 3rd fingers on E♭

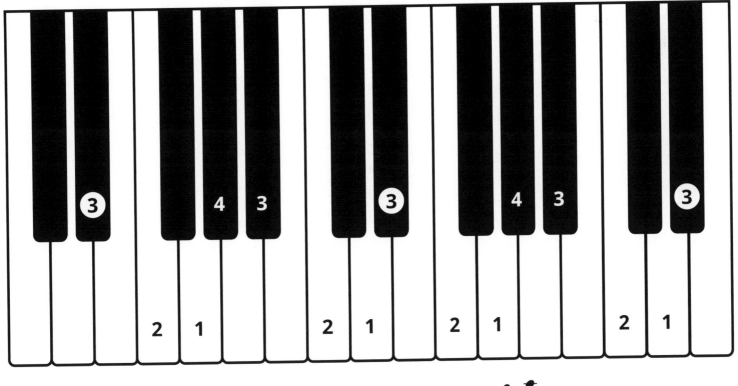

LH

B♭ major

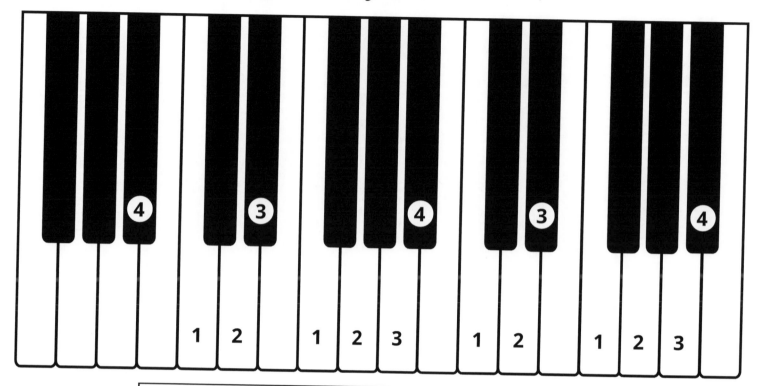

Opposite 3rd and 4th fingers on B♭ and E♭

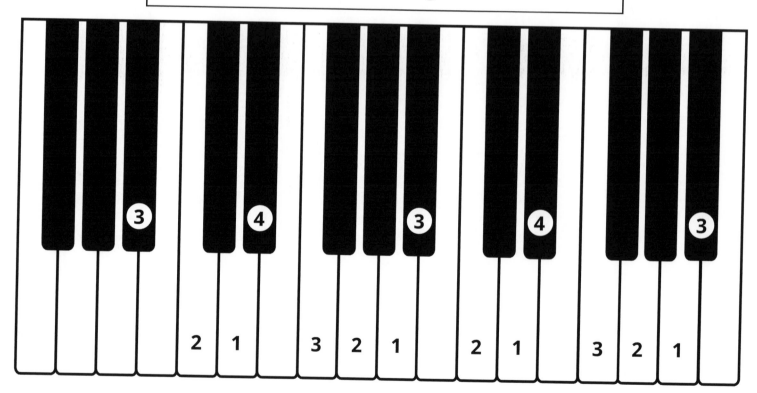

Minor Scales
Group 4

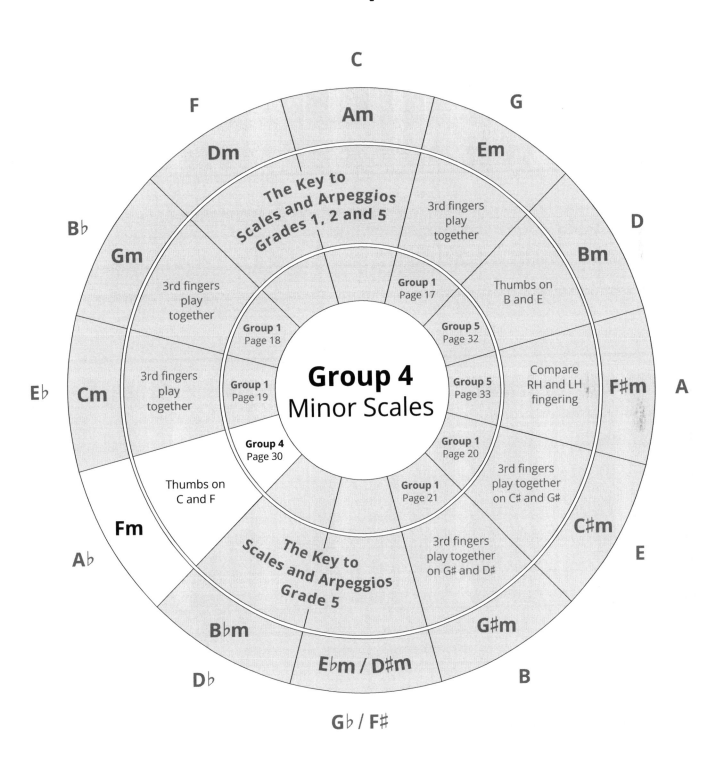

F harmonic minor

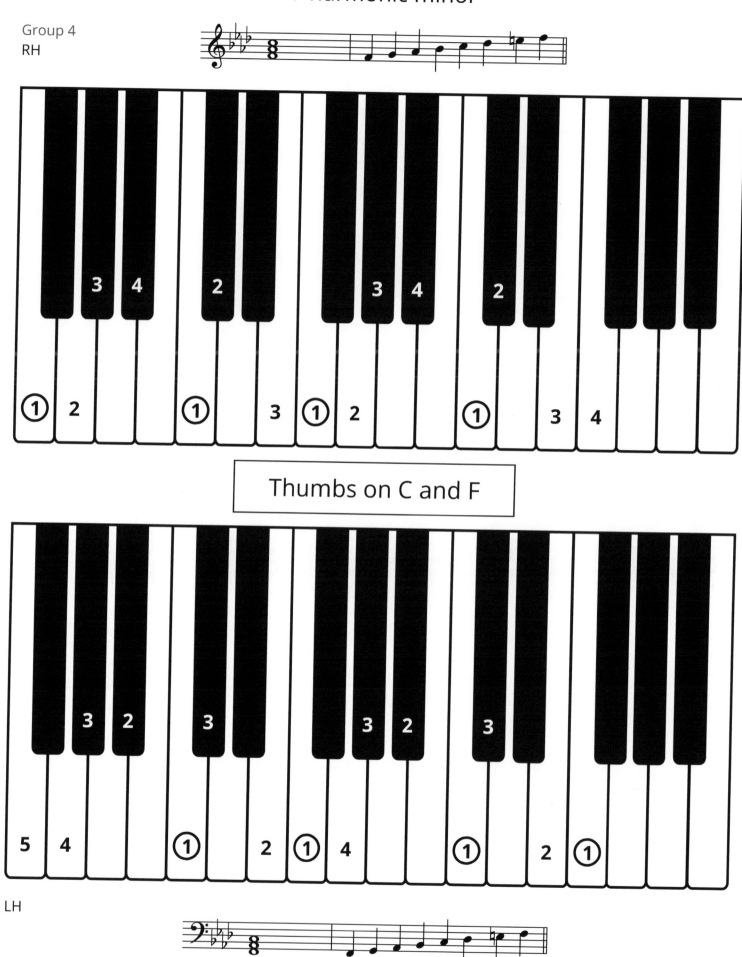

Thumbs on C and F

Minor Scales
Group 5

C

F

G

Am

Dm

Em

B♭

D

Gm

Bm

The Key to
Scales and Arpeggios
Grades 1, 2 and 5

3rd fingers
play
together

3rd fingers
play
together

Group 1
Page 17

Thumbs on
B and E

Group 1
Page 18

Group 5
Page 32

E♭

Cm

3rd fingers
play
together

Group 1
Page 19

Group 5
Page 33

Compare
RH and LH
fingering

F♯m

A

Group 4
Page 30

Group 1
Page 20

Group 5
Minor Scales

Fm

Thumbs on
C and F

Group 1
Page 21

3rd fingers
play together
on C♯ and G♯

C♯m

A♭

The Key to
Scales and Arpeggios
Grade 5

3rd fingers
play together
on G♯ and D♯

E

B♭m

G♯m

D♭

E♭m / D♯m

B

G♭ / F♯

B harmonic minor

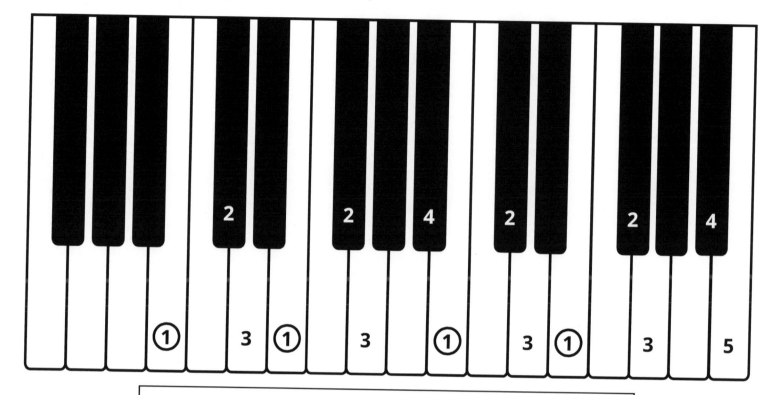

Thumbs on B and E

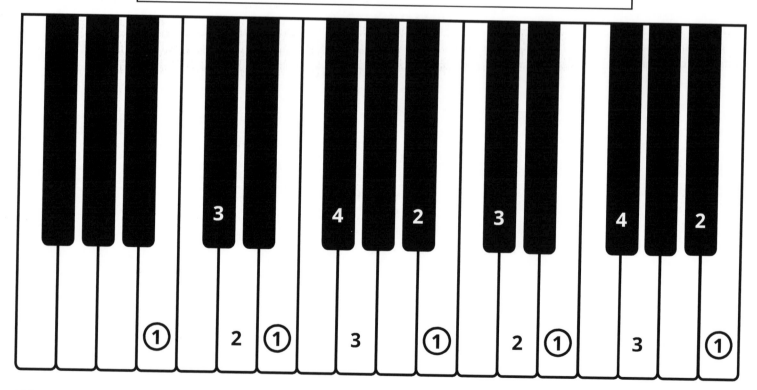

LH

F# minor

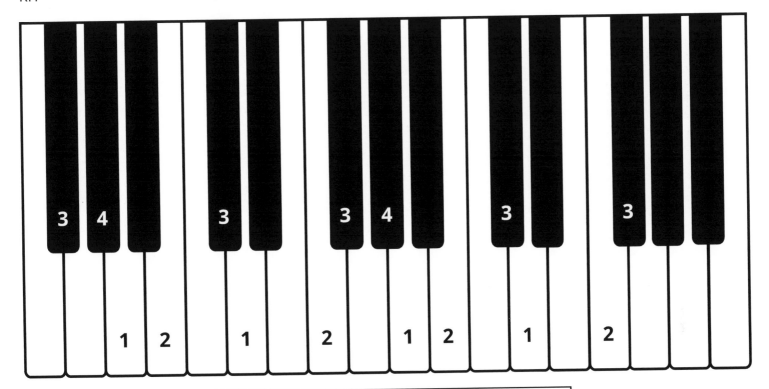

Compare RH and LH fingering

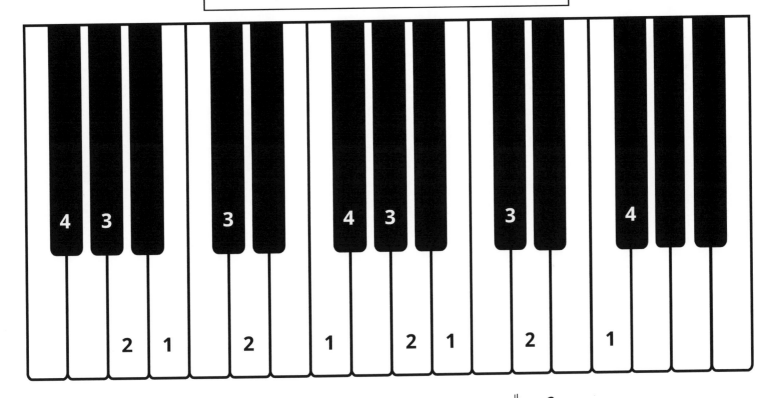

LH

Arpeggios

Remember:

B **major** chord:	B	D#	F#
B **minor** chord:	B	D♮	F#

Tips:

- Begin by playing the chord and think of the note names.
- The middle note moves down a semitone from major to minor.

A choice of LH 3rd or 4th finger is illustrated.

As the 4th finger tends to be weaker, try practising with the LH 3rd finger for major arpeggios and 4th finger for minor arpeggios. This also helps to distinguish between the major and minor keys.

Major Arpeggios
Group 1

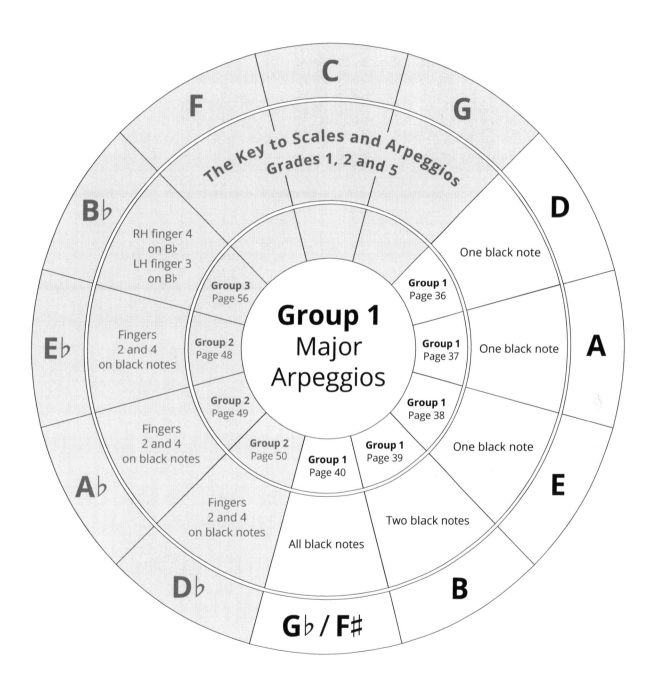

The Key to Scales and Arpeggios
Grades 1, 2 and 5

Group 1
Major
Arpeggios

F

C

G

D

A

E

B

Gb / F#

Db

Ab

Eb

Bb

RH finger 4
on Bb
LH finger 3
on Bb

Fingers
2 and 4
on black notes

Fingers
2 and 4
on black notes

Fingers
2 and 4
on black notes

All black notes

Two black notes

One black note

One black note

One black note

Group 3
Page 56

Group 2
Page 48

Group 2
Page 49

Group 2
Page 50

Group 1
Page 40

Group 1
Page 39

Group 1
Page 38

Group 1
Page 37

Group 1
Page 36

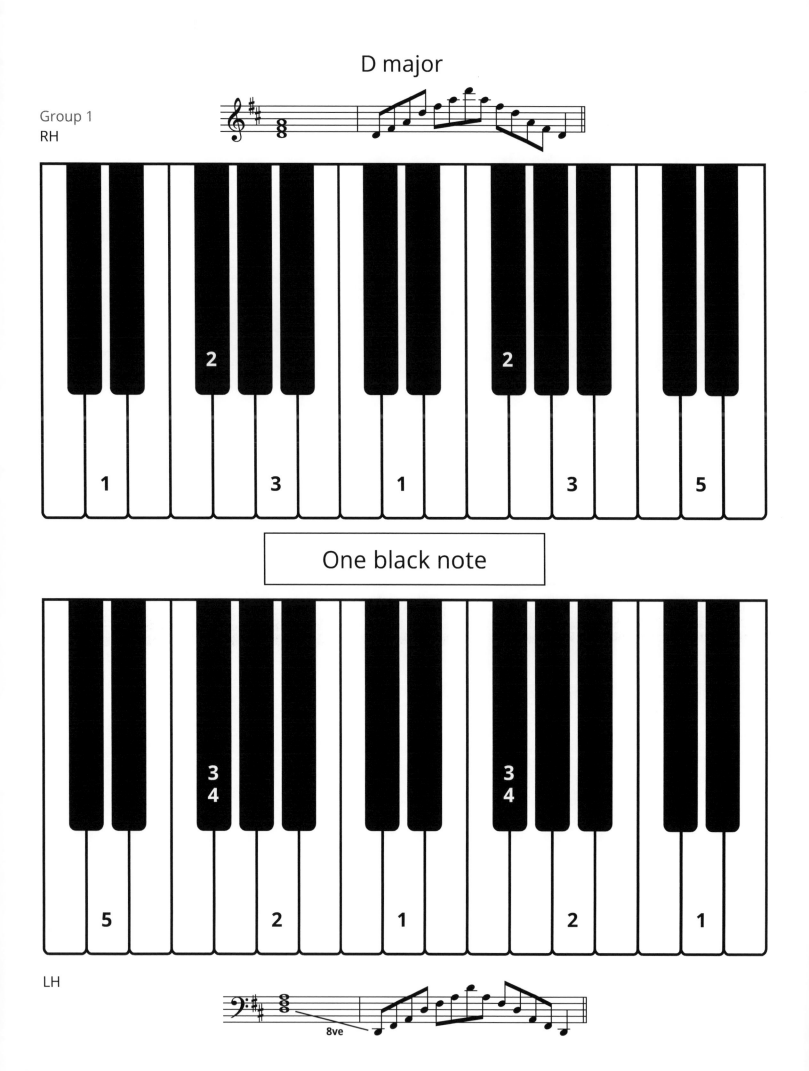

D major

Group 1
RH

One black note

LH

A major

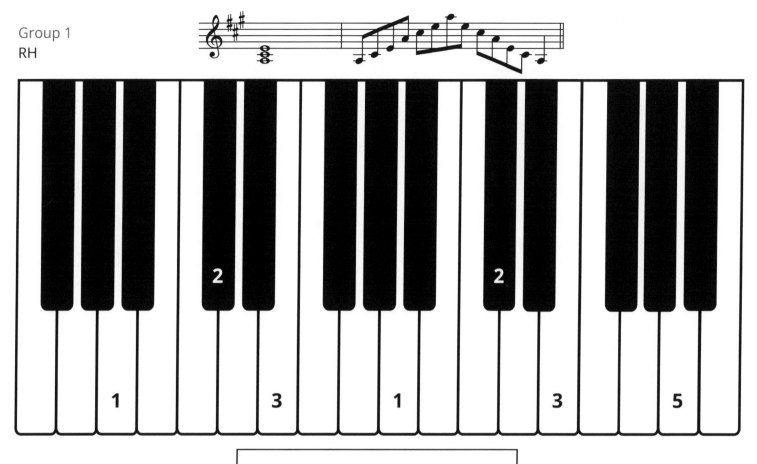

One black note

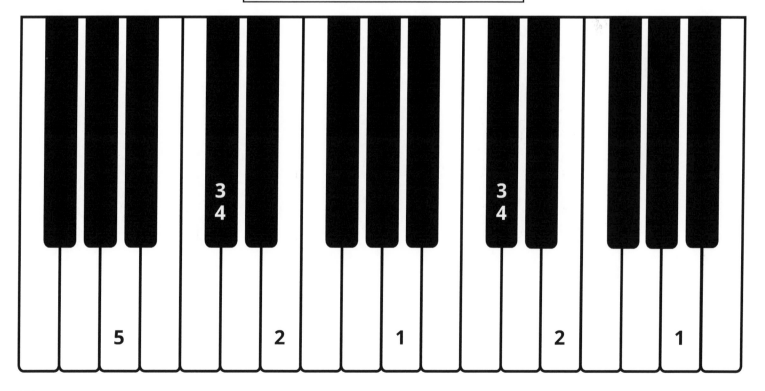

LH

E major

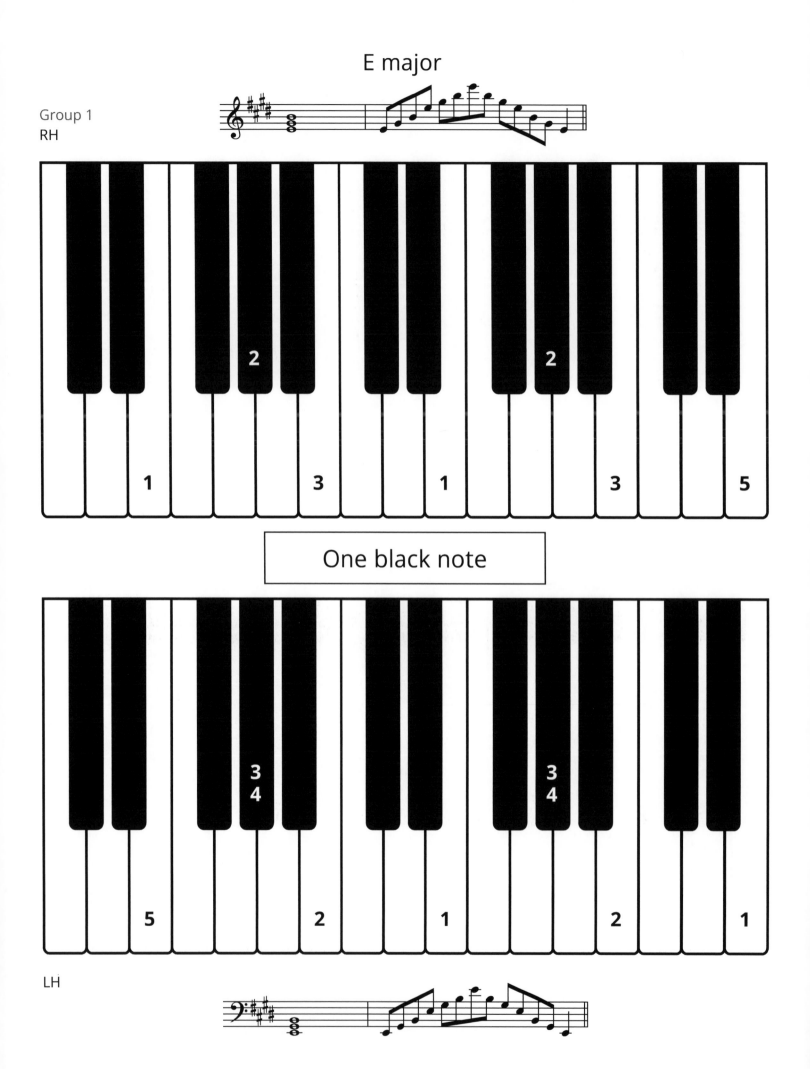

One black note

B major

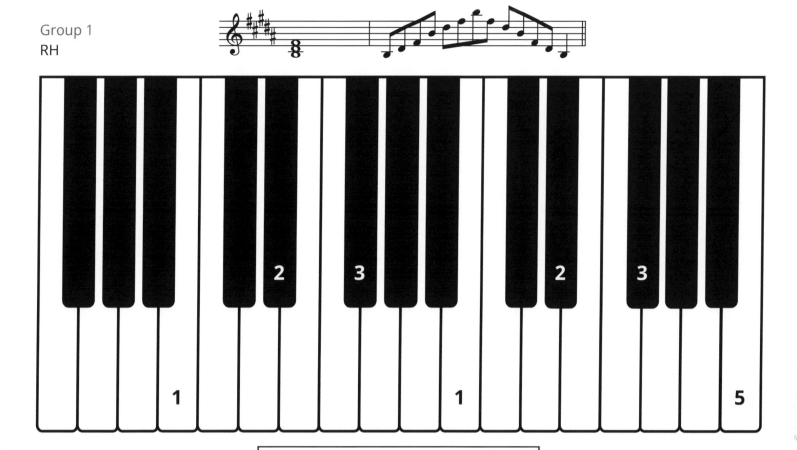

Two black notes

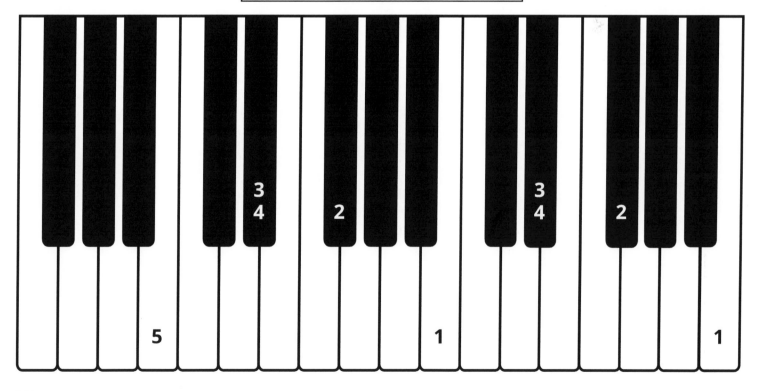

LH

F♯ major

Group 1
RH

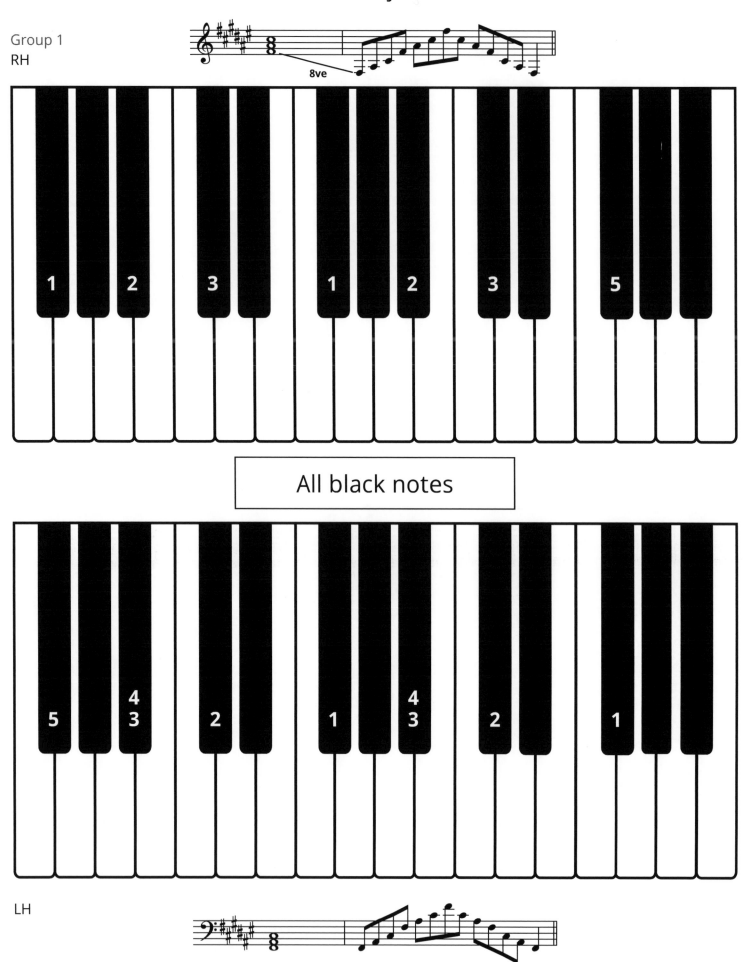

All black notes

LH

Minor Arpeggios
Group 1

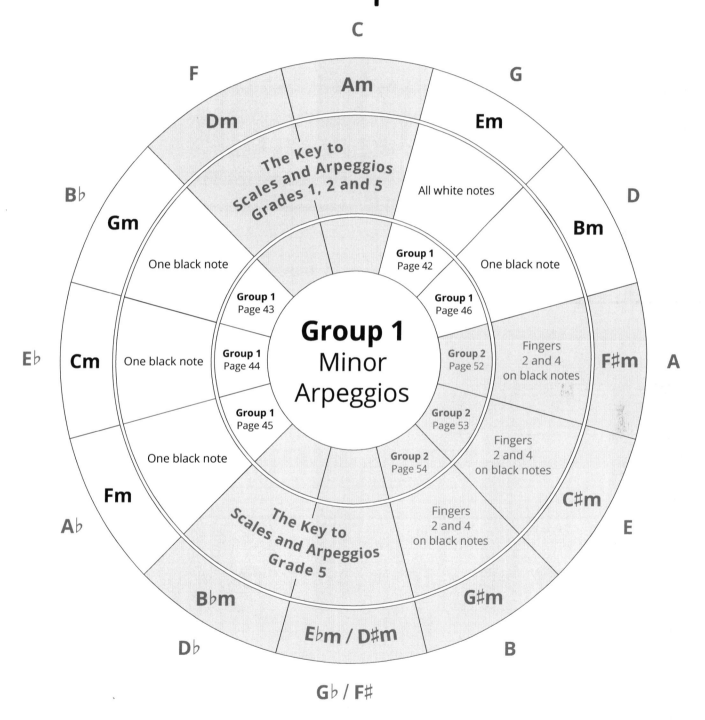

E minor

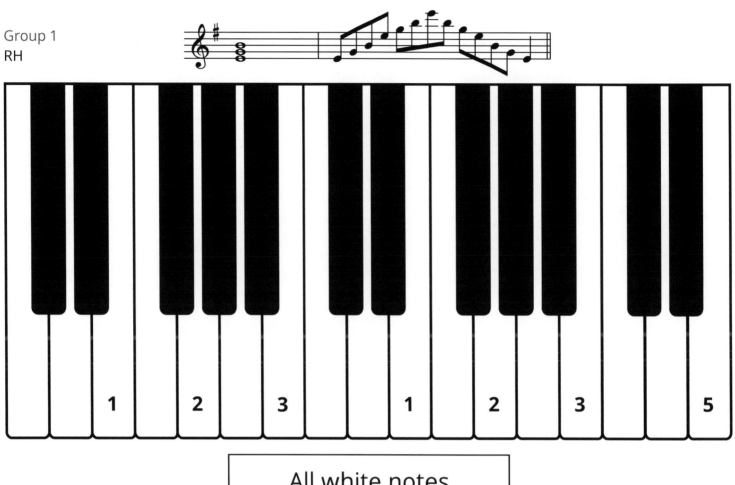

All white notes

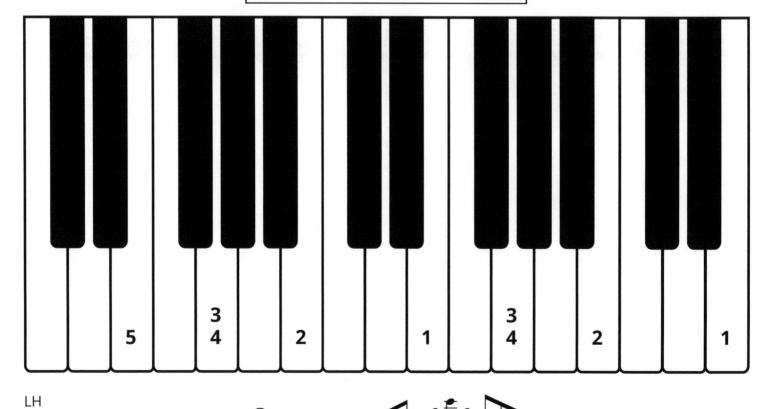

LH

G minor

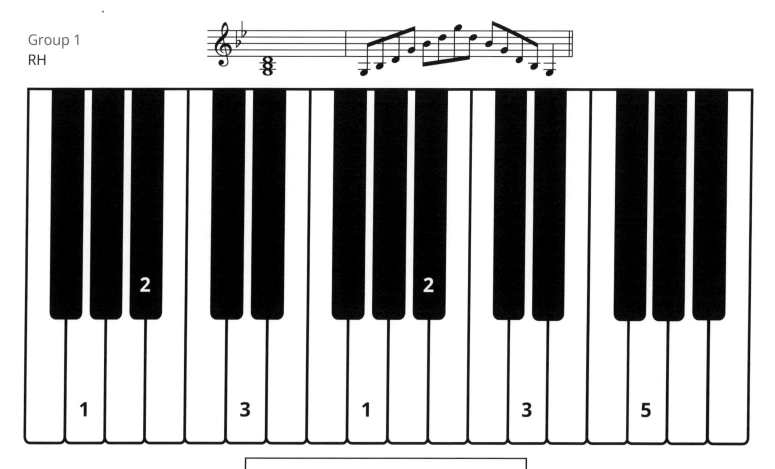

One black note

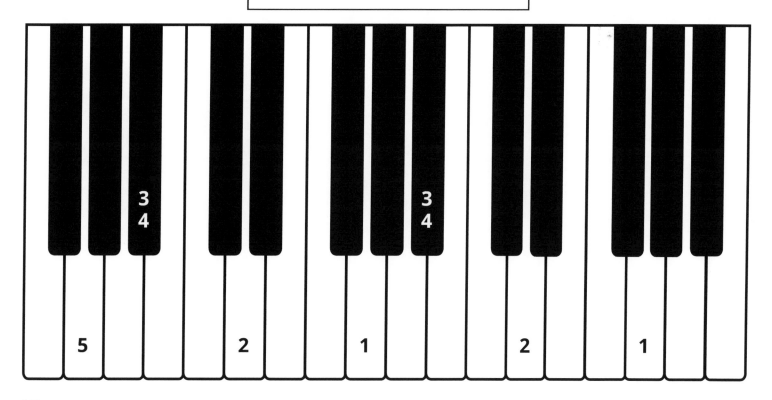

LH

C minor

Group 1
RH

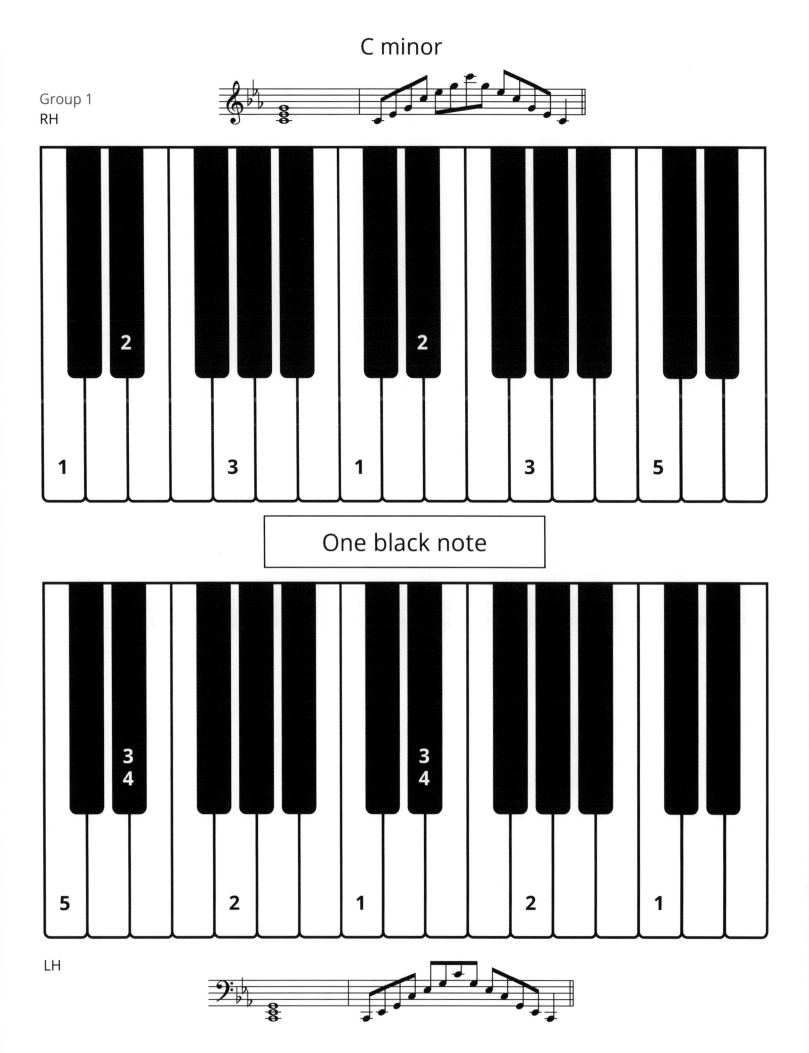

One black note

LH

F minor

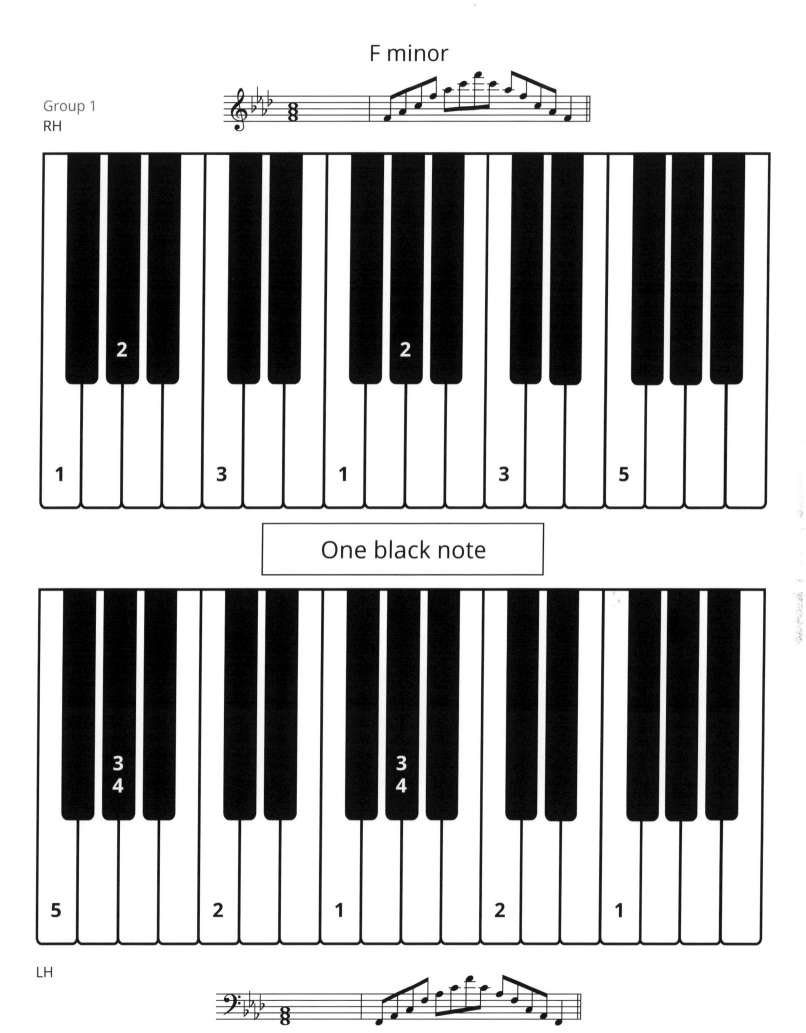

One black note

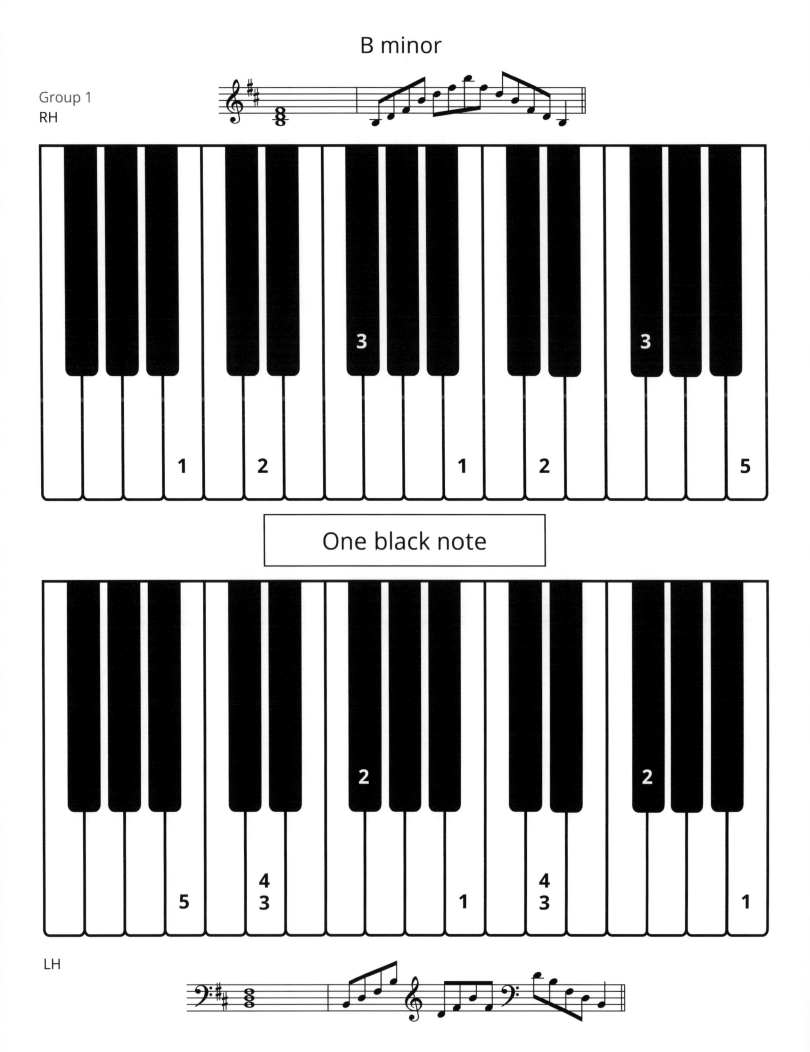

Major Arpeggios
Group 2

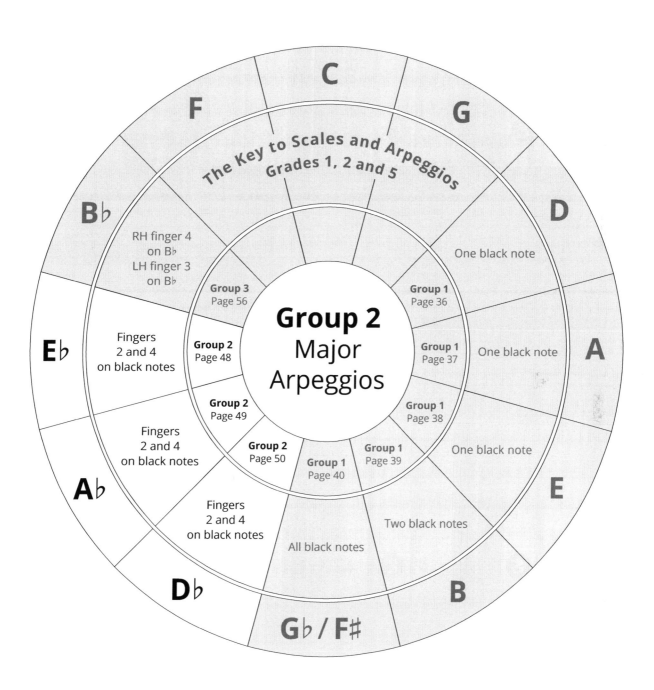

E♭ major

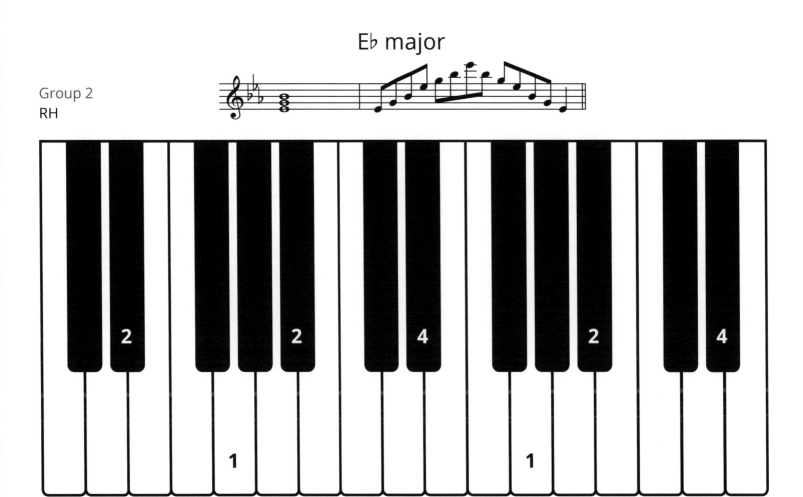

Fingers 2 and 4 on black notes

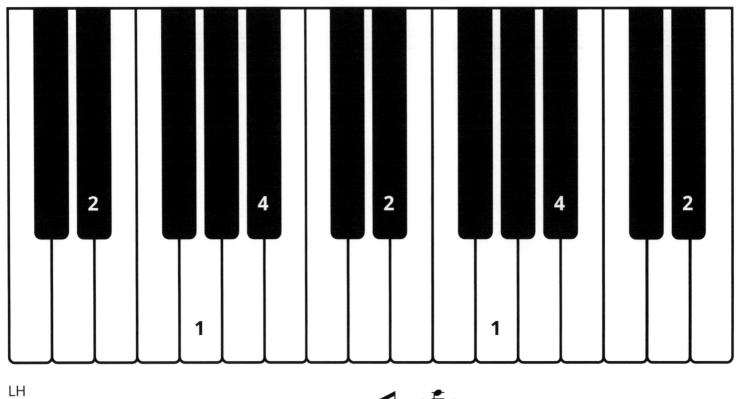

A♭ major

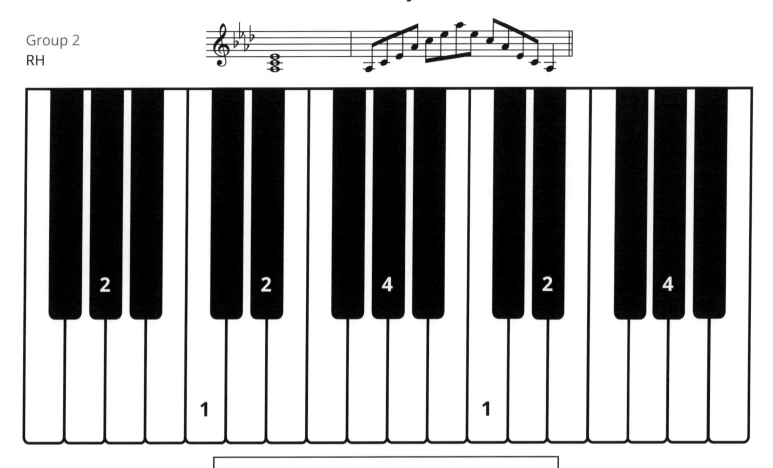

Fingers 2 and 4 on black notes

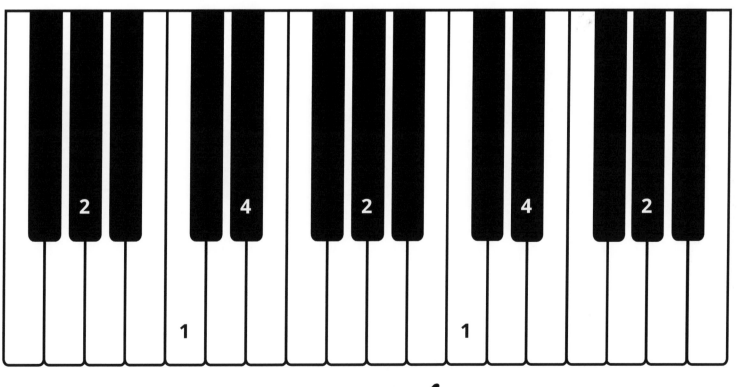

LH

D♭ major

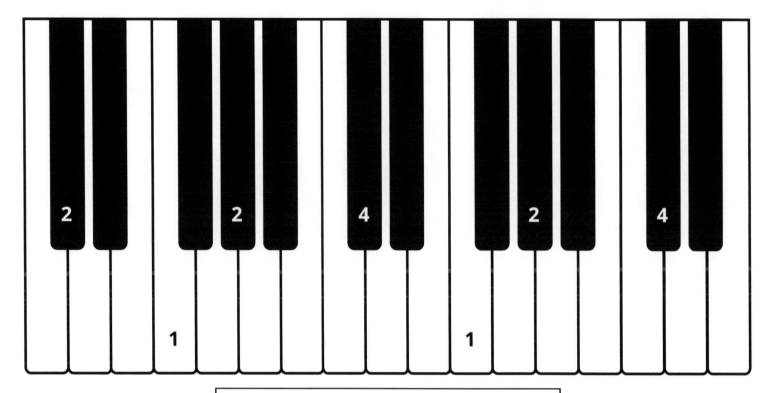

Fingers 2 and 4 on black notes

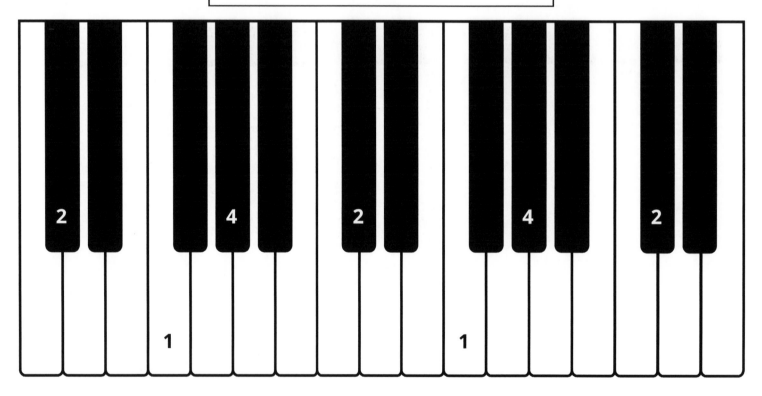

LH

Minor Arpeggios
Group 2

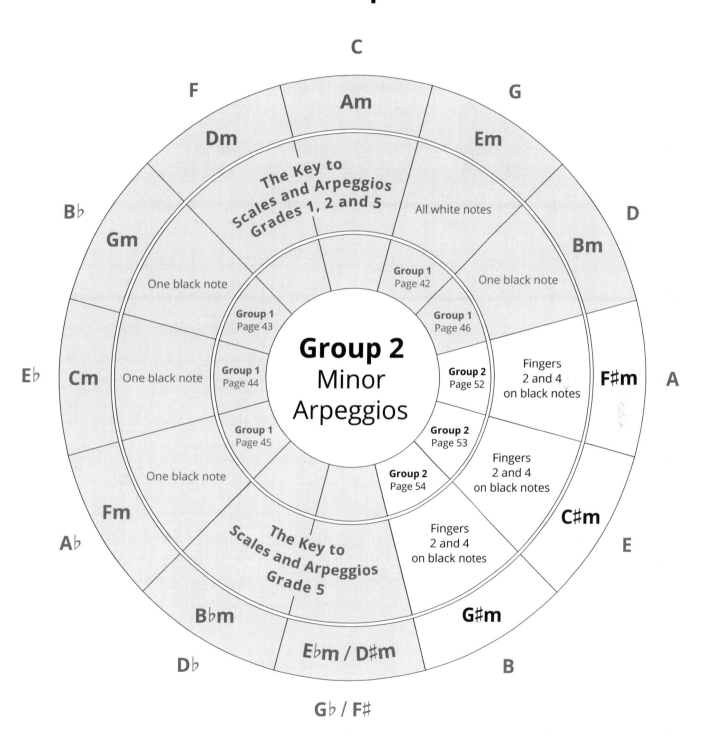

F♯ minor

Group 2
RH

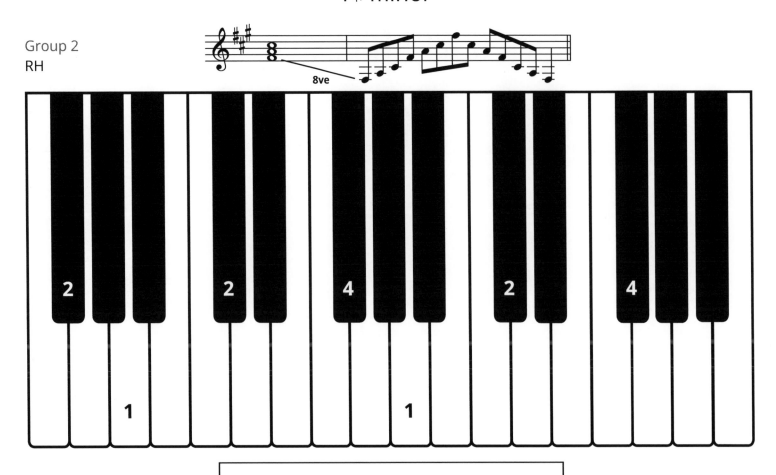

Fingers 2 and 4 on black notes

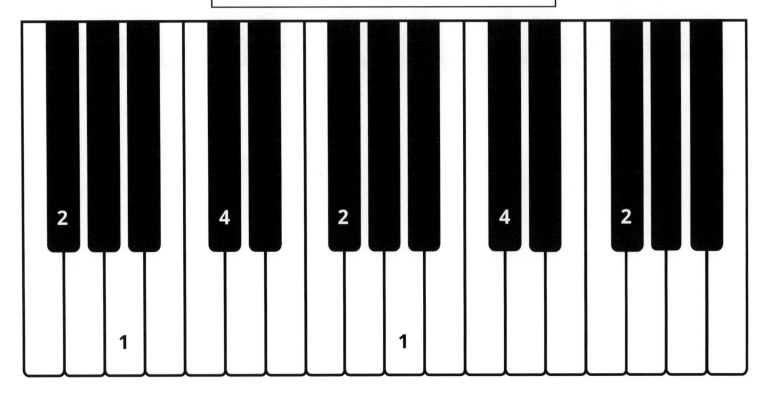

LH

Enharmonic D#

Group 2
RH

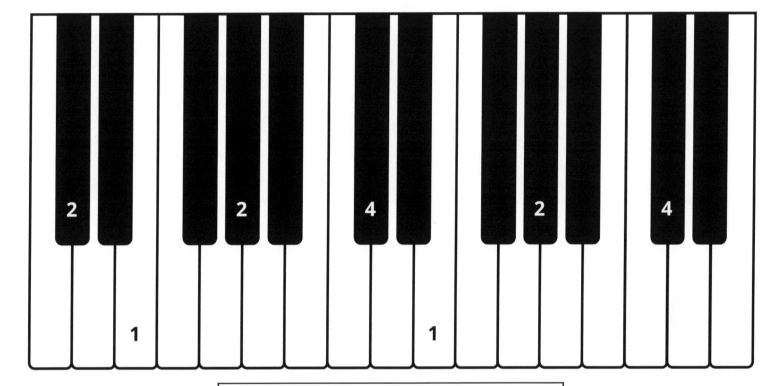

Fingers 2 and 4 on black notes

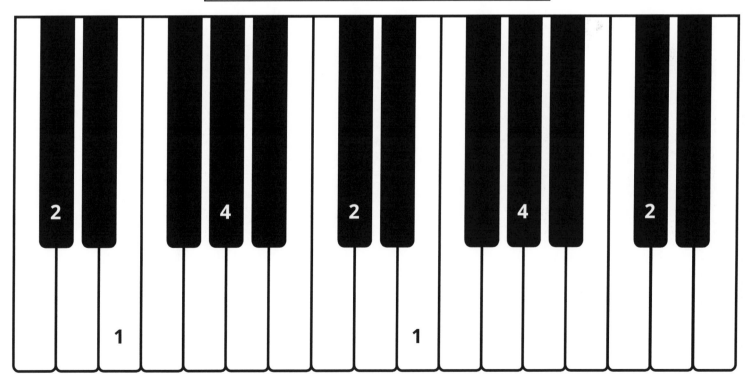

LH

Enharmonic A♭

G♯ minor

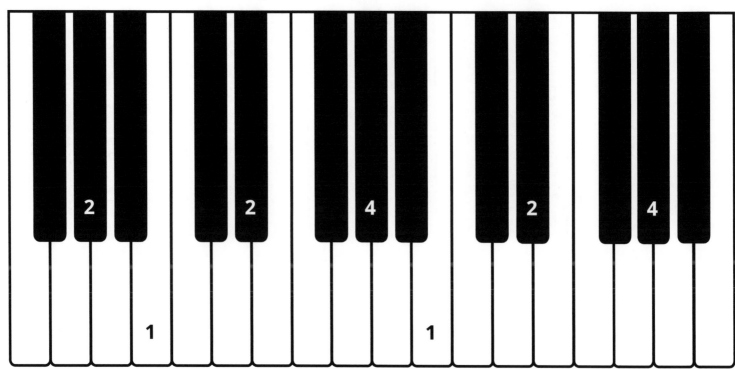

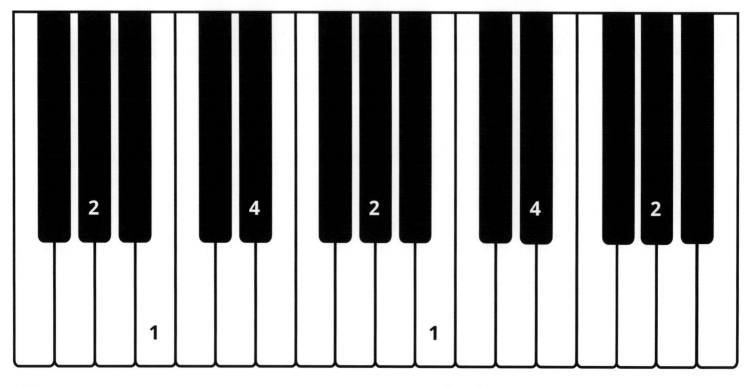

Fingers 2 and 4 on black notes

Major Arpeggios
Group 3

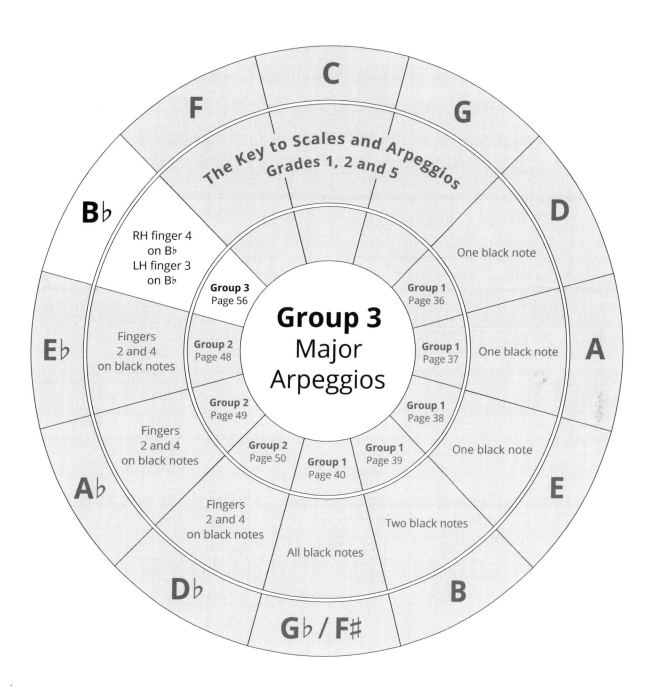

B♭ major

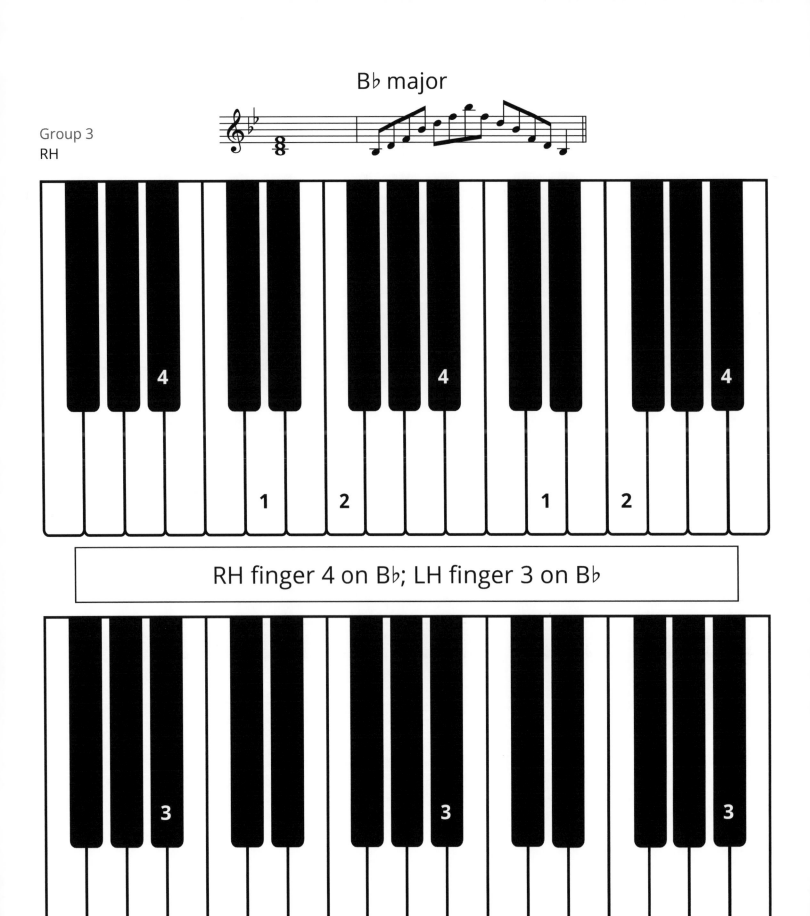

RH finger 4 on B♭; LH finger 3 on B♭

LH

Chromatic Scales

The basic fingering, 1,3,1,3,1,2,3 is illustrated as well as two further patterns which will strengthen fingers 4 and 5 and enable much faster playing once they are mastered.

Pattern 1
This fingering repeats every two octaves.

Pattern 2
Chopin fingering using finger 3 on black notes and fingers 4 and 5 on each pair of consecutive white notes.

This is the fingering illustrated in Etude no 2 Opus 10.

Chromatic scale in similar motion

Basic fingering

RH

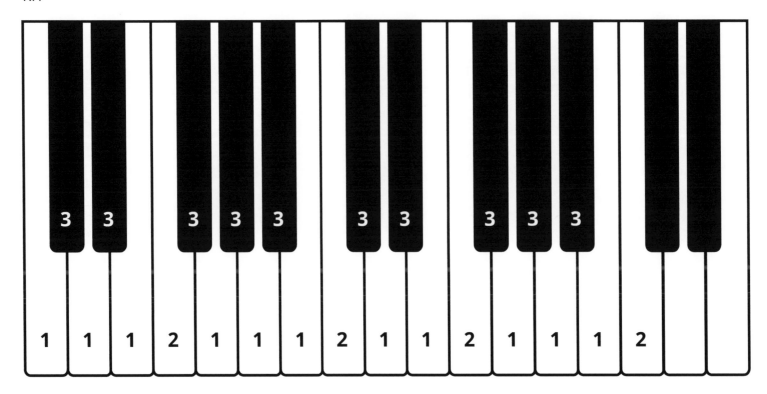

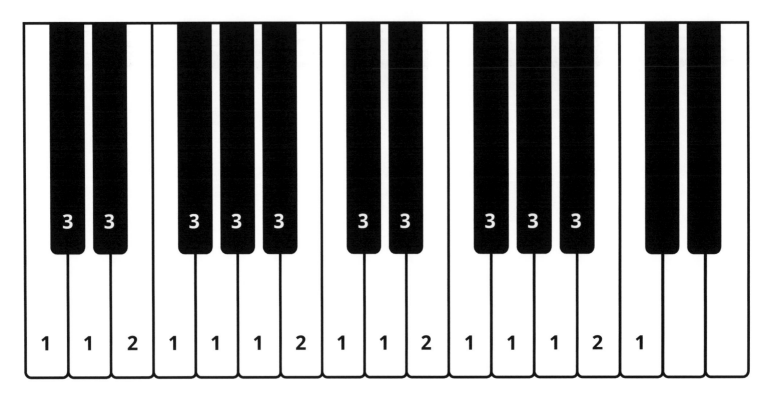

LH

Chromatic scale in similar motion

Pattern 1

RH

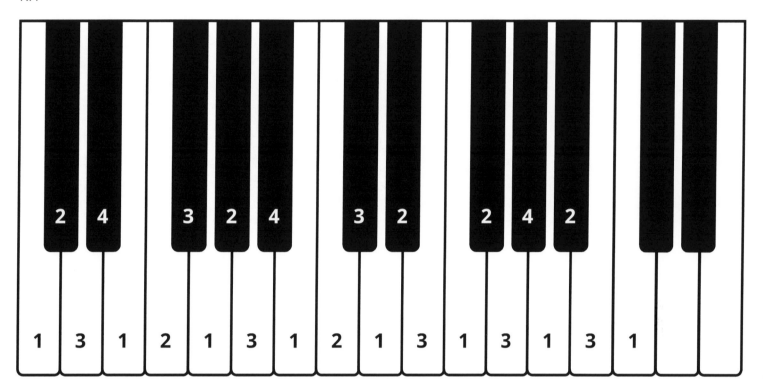

LH

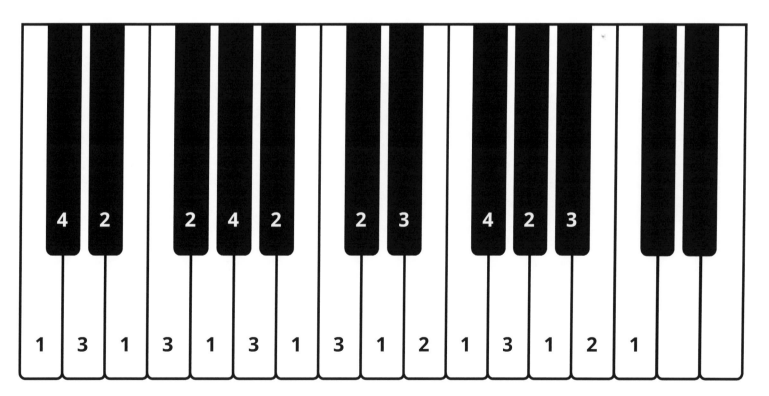

Chopin fingering as in Etude no 2 Opus 10

Pattern 2

RH

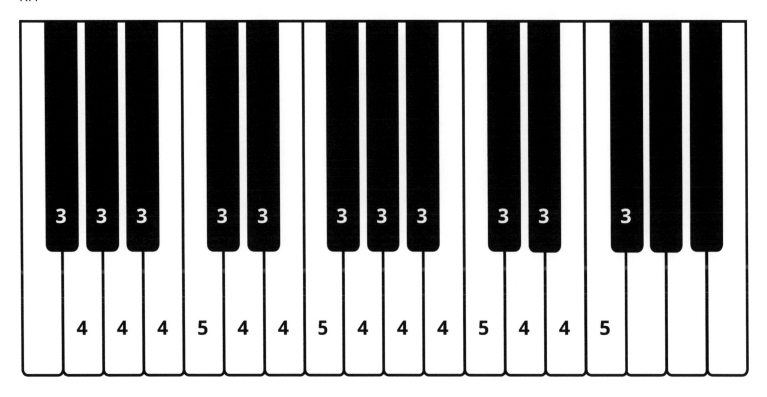

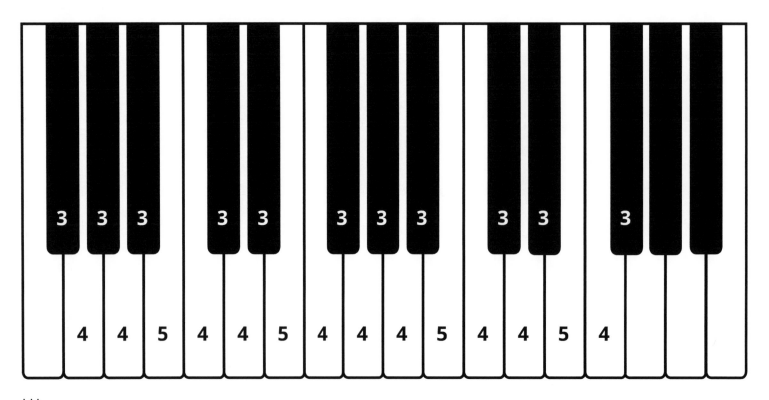

LH

Chromatic scale in contrary motion beginning on D

Pattern 1

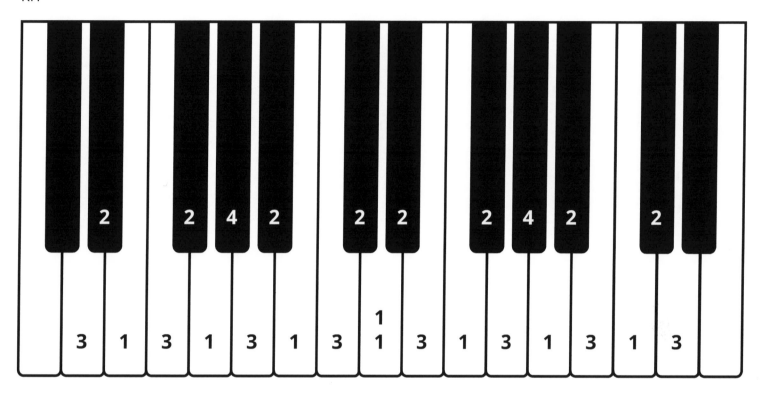

Chromatic scale in contrary motion beginning on A♭

Pattern 2

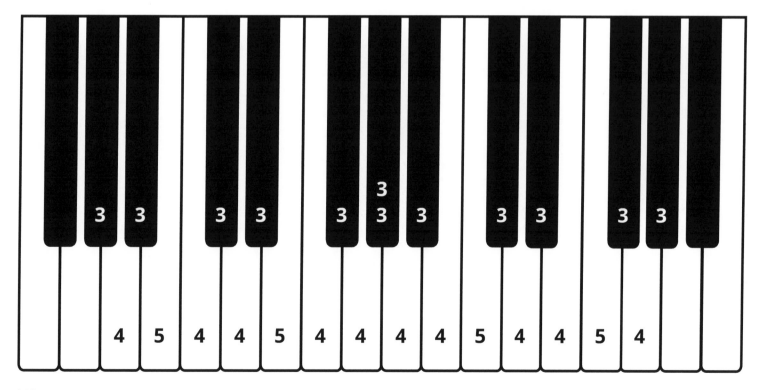

Contrary Motion Scales

E major	C# minor
E♭ major	C minor

Tips:

- Firstly, **look** at the keyboard diagram without playing.
- Compare both black note and white note fingering.
- Learn the first four notes, hands together, of each scale. This will give you confidence, especially in the minor scales.
- For E♭ major think:
  'black, white white, black black, white white, black' etc. Sing as you play!

E major

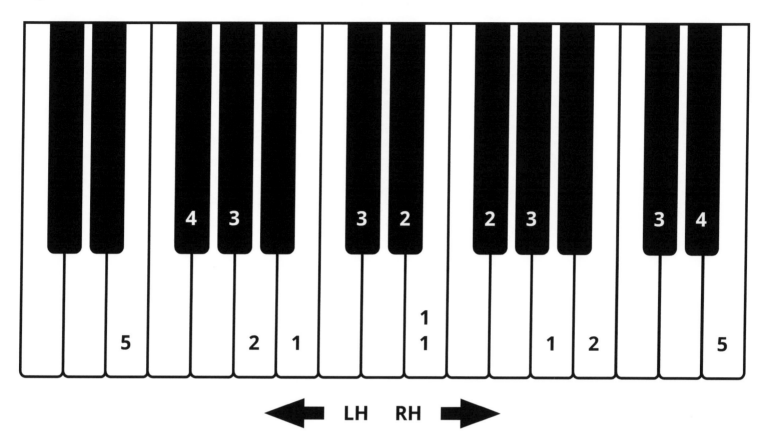

C# minor

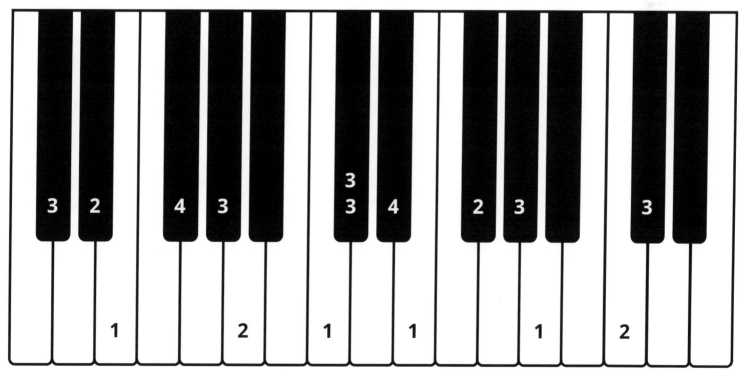

Eb major

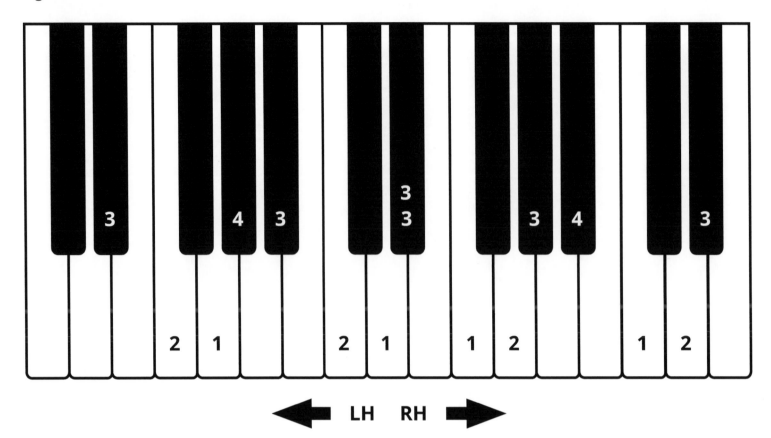

C minor

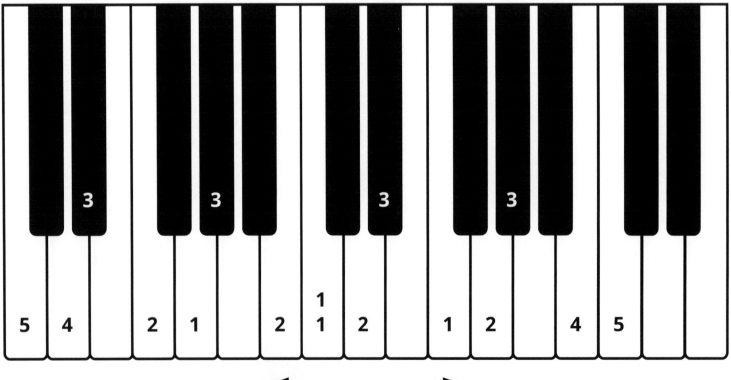

Index

Scales

Arpeggios

Chromatic Scales

Contrary Motion Scales